Organizational Behavior

John Middleton

T0313612

- Fast track route to understanding and managing human behavior in organizations

- Covers the key areas of OB, from understanding individual and group behavior patterns and attitudes to work to building successful organizations and improving your personal effectiveness in the workplace

- Examples and lessons from some of the world's most successful businesses, including Tesco, Sears, Sundaram-Clayton and The Natural Step, and ideas from the smartest thinkers including Charles Handy, Jack Wood, Edgar Schein and Shoshana Zuboff

- Includes a glossary of key concepts and a comprehensive resources guide

ORGANIZATIONS

07.10

>>EXPRESSEXEC.COM<<
essential management thinking at your fingertips

The right of John Middleton to be identified as the author of this work has been asserted in accordance with the Copyright, Designs and Patents Act 1988

First published 2002 by
Capstone Publishing (a Wiley company)
8 Newtec Place
Magdalen Road
Oxford OX4 1RE
United Kingdom
http://www.capstoneideas.com

CIP catalogue records for this book are available from the British Library and the US Library of Congress

ISBN 1-84112-217-3

Substantial discounts on bulk quantities of Capstone books are available to corporations, professional associations and other organizations. Please contact Capstone for more details on +44 (0)1865 798 623 or (fax) (0)1865 240 941 or (e-mail) info@wiley-capstone.co.uk

+44

MIX
Paper from
responsible sources
FSC   FSC® C013604
www.fsc.org

Contents

Introduction to ExpressExec

ExpressExec is 3 million words of the latest management thinking compiled into 10 modules. Each module contains 10 individual titles forming a comprehensive resource of current business practice written by leading practitioners in their field. From brand management to balanced scorecard, ExpressExec enables you to grasp the key concepts behind each subject and implement the theory immediately. Each of the 100 titles is available in print and electronic formats.

Through the ExpressExec.com Website you will discover that you can access the complete resource in a number of ways:

» printed books or e-books;
» e-content – PDF or XML (for licensed syndication) adding value to an intranet or Internet site;
» a corporate e-learning/knowledge management solution providing a cost-effective platform for developing skills and sharing knowledge within an organization;
» bespoke delivery – tailored solutions to solve your need.

Why not visit www.expressexec.com and register for free key management briefings, a monthly newsletter and interactive skills checklists. Share your ideas about ExpressExec and your thoughts about business today.

Please contact elound@wiley-capstone.co.uk for more information.

Introduction

» The field of organizational behavior (OB) draws from the behavioral science disciplines of psychology, social psychology, and cultural anthropology.

» The areas on which OB focuses are *individuals* who will often be working within *groups*, which themselves work within *organizations*.

» OB is as much a practical set of tools as an area of theoretical interest.

"Smirk all you like about the Organization Man; his trade-off made possible the 30-year mortgages and college educations that the great American dream was historically made of ... the old understanding is dead. Interred with it is much of the conventional wisdom on retaining and motivating the American worker."[1]

New York Times *staff writer Mary Williams Walsh*

An organization is more than a formal arrangement of functions, more than an organization chart, more than a vision statement, more than a set of accounts. An organization consists of people and so it is also a social system.

In this book, we will be looking at and seeking to explain human behavior within organizations. The field of organizational behavior (OB) draws primarily from the behavioral science disciplines of psychology, social psychology, and cultural anthropology. The areas on which OB focuses are *individuals* who will often be working within *groups*, which themselves work within *organizations*, as well as all the inter-relationships between them. Some of the specific themes embraced by OB are personality theory, attitudes and values, motivation and learning, interpersonal behavior, group dynamics, leadership and team-work, organizational structure and design, decision-making, power, conflict, and negotiation. Some OB thinkers go further and suggest that the behavior within the organization has to be viewed partly in the wider context of the outside world's effect on the organization and its human resources, missions, objectives, and strategies.

These are not merely areas of theoretical interest. They underpin practical organizational activities. A discussion with an underper-forming team member requires an understanding of individual moti-vation; running an effective meeting needs an appreciation of group dynamics; dealing with colleagues, suppliers, or customers from another country calls on a sensitivity to cultural differences; helping two team members to resolve a difference can involve conflict resolution and negotiation skills; and so on.

To complicate matters further, OB is not a static field. Just look at what's happened to the world of work over the past century or so and think about how attitudes to, behavior at, and expectations of work have changed. Mass production; the rise of "organization man''; management by objective; the technological explosion of the 1960s; personal computers; the decline of manufacturing; business process re-engineering; outsourcing; downshifting; portfolio workers; globalization; the fall of "organization man" amid a dramatic fall in job tenure; the "war for talent"; the ascent and descent of the dot-coms; all have impacted on organizational thinking and individual behavior over the years.

In this book, you'll find a broad overview of OB's key themes, as well as some practical guidance on how you might improve your personal effectiveness in the workplace. There's also a section on resources, which will point you towards sources of further information that will help you explore in greater depth. You won't find answers to all the human issues that confront the modern organization, but you should find plenty to reinforce that well-used cliché from many an annual report: that a company's most precious asset is its people.

NOTE

1 Walsh, M.W. (2001) *New York Times*, 6 April.

Definition of Terms

» What is *organizational behavior*? One definition: "The study of the structure, functioning and performance of organizations, and the behavior of groups and individuals within them."
» Key areas of focus are *individuals*, *groups*, and the whole *organization*, and the interplay between them.
» *Macro* OB is a pre-occupation with the "organization" in organizational behavior; *micro* OB is a pre-occupation with the "behavior." Different levels can be used for analyzing organizational issues.

"Organizations are social arrangements, constructed by people who can also change them. Organizations can be repressive and stifling, but they can also be designed to provide opportunities for self-fulfillment and individual expression. The point is that human consequences depend on how organizations are designed and run."[1]

David Buchanan and Andrzej Huczynski

"Organizations are a system of co-operative activities – and their co-ordination requires something intangible and personal that is largely a matter of personal relationships."[2]

Chester Barnard

There are a number of definitions that we can draw on to illuminate and deepen our understanding of the concept of organizational behavior.

One of the earliest, and certainly one of the most succinct definitions, comes from Derek Pugh, who in 1970 was appointed by London Business School to the position of Chair in Organizational Behavior, the first appointment of its kind in Great Britain. According to Pugh, OB is concerned with "the study of the structure, functioning and performance of organizations, and the behavior of groups and individuals within them."[3]

John Ivancevich and Michael Matteson, in their book *Organizational Behavior and Management*, offer a broader definition. They say that OB is about:

"the study of human behavior, attitudes and performance within an organizational setting; drawing on theory, methods, and principles from such disciplines as psychology, sociology, and cultural anthropology to learn about individual perception, values, learning capabilities, and actions while working with groups and within the total organization; analyzing the external environment's effect on the organization and its human resources, missions, objectives and strategies."[4]

What emerges from these two definitions is a view of OB as:

» A way of thinking
» An interdisciplinary field

» Having a distinctly humanistic outlook
» Performance oriented
» Seeing the external environment as critical
» Using scientific method
» Having an applications orientation.

Not everybody is convinced that OB represents a coherent field. Jack Wood is a professor of Organizational Behavior at IMD/Lausanne. In a contribution to a book called *Mastering Management*, he writes as follows:

> "Management textbooks frequently state as fact that organizational behavior is a interdisciplinary field. It is not. It is in no way interdisciplinary; multidisciplinary perhaps, but not interdisciplinary. OB is not a coherent field. It is a general area that encompasses thinking and research from numerous disciplines and subdisciplines ... Organizational behavior is in reality a hodgepodge of various subjects; a collection of loosely related or even unrelated streams of scholarly and not-so-scholarly research. It is neither a discipline nor is it a business function. And that makes it an anomalous area of management study."[5]

In an effort to reduce the complexity and breadth of organizational behavior, Wood makes a useful distinction between what he calls *macro* OB and *micro* OB.

Macro OB, he says, is "a preoccupation of those with interests in formal organizations and structural questions" whereas micro OB is concerned with "informal organizations and individual and small group questions." Another way of looking at it is to think of macro OB as a pre-occupation with the "organization" in organizational behavior and micro OB as a pre-occupation with the "behavior" in organizational behavior.

OB VS. OD

In defining the concept of Organizational Behavior, which has been around since the 1960s, it is useful to acknowledge that a similar term – Organization Development (OD for short) – has been around for just as long.

One of the most widely-used definitions of OD appears in a 1969 book by Richard Beckhard.[6] He writes that OD:

> "is an effort that is planned, organization-wide, and managed from the top, to increase organizational effectiveness and health, through planned interventions in the organization's 'processes,' using behavioral-science knowledge."

OB and OD started out from different bases – with OB focusing on behavior within companies and OD concentrating on processes – but over the years their territories have overlapped to the extent that many people now treat the two terms as virtually interchangeable.

LEVELS OF ANALYSIS

Wood offers a very useful model for exploring behavioral events. He suggests that different levels of analysis can be applied when examining the significance of an organizational issue. He proposes eight, namely:

1 Individual
2 Team
3 Intergroup
4 Organizational
5 Interorganizational
6 Societal
7 International
8 Global.

Let's take a quick example. Say there was a new member of your team at work who attended the corporate induction program, but who is underperforming – how might you account for their lower than expected level of performance? Depending on how you viewed that individual and who you listened to, here are some of the reasons you might come up with.

» They just don't have the brains for the job (that is, the problem lies at the *Individual* level).

» Their colleagues are not being supportive (in which case this is a *Team* level problem).
» The induction program prepared by the Training department was of poor quality on this occasion (indicating an *Intergroup* problem).
» The company's training budget has been slashed (which is an *Organizational* issue).

And so on. Why does this matter? The point is that the level of explanation that we choose determines our view of the causes of an event or problem. It also affects the actions that we take, and the solutions that we employ. In an organization, inappropriate intervention at the wrong level can make a problem worse rather than better.

Here are three further points to consider:

» People tend to pick their favorite level of analysis to explain events, and then behave accordingly. This is often particularly true of external consultants brought in to perform a "quick fix."
» People are most familiar with, and often prefer, explanations at the individual level of behavior. Trying to change people by sending them on a training course is simpler than changing structures or upgrading technology. However, such explanations are often too simplistic, inaccurate, or incomplete.
» As a general principle, any organizational problem can be usefully analyzed at ever-higher levels of abstraction. By considering a problem progressively at the individual, group, intergroup, and organizational levels, a deeper understanding of its causes can be gained. As a result, the tools needed to tackle the problem can be chosen more accurately, and applied more effectively.

Looking at a problem systemically will always yield a better understanding than simply leaping in with fixed preconceptions. So in future, before you blame a member of staff for mixing up a customer's order, maybe you need to ask yourself whether it truly was their fault.

PULLING IT ALL TOGETHER

Organizational Behavior is characterized by a view that organizations can be best explored by approaching them from a range of different perspectives. Just as there is no one best way to run and organize a business, so there is no one best perspective from which a total understanding of organizations can be gained.

OB draws its strength from its richness and variety of perspectives. Although this can lead commentators like Jack Wood to describe OB as a "hodgepodge," this is also its greatest source of strength. The trick of it, of course, is to detect which particular approach to a given organizational issue might best suit your particular company with its unique culture and at a specific moment in its corporate history. Make the right choice and OB will deliver.

NOTES

1 Buchanan, D. & Huczynski, A. (1997) *Organizational Behaviour: An Introductory Text*, 3rd edn, Prentice Hall, London.
2 Barnard, C.I. (1938) *Functions of the Executive*, Harvard University Press, Cambridge, MA.
3 Pugh, D. (1971) *Organization Theory: Selected Readings*, Penguin, Harmondsworth.
4 Ivancevich, J. & Matteson, M. (1998) *Organizational Behaviour and Management*, 3rd edn, Irwin, Chicago and London.
5 Wood, J. (1997) in Dickson, T. & Bickerstaffe, G. (eds.) *Mastering Management: The Definitive Guide to the Foundations and Frontiers of Finance*, FT/Pitman Publishing, London.
6 Beckhard, R. (1969) *Organization Development: Strategies and Models*, Addison-Wesley, Reading, MA.

The Evolution of Organizational Behavior

» Henry Fayol's principles of management.
» Scientific management: Frederick Taylor.
» The Human Relations Movement.
» 1950 to the present day.
» A brief history of organizational theory.
» Landmark publications on Organizational Behaviour.

"Man has two sets of needs. His need as an animal to avoid pain and his need as a human to grow psychologically"[1]

Frederick Herzberg

"The hierarchy is under siege because it's increasingly inefficient and many of the most effective workers in our companies are sick of it. They're tired of the rituals, the lack of real communication, the delays in making decisions and taking actions. With new technology diffusing information widely, many feel that the issue isn't who you are in the structure but what you want to get accomplished."[2]

D. Quinn Mills

A BRIEF HISTORY OF ORGANIZATIONAL BEHAVIOR – THE IMPOSSIBLE DREAM

As mentioned before, some of the specific themes embraced by Organizational Behavior are: personality theory; attitudes and values; motivation and learning; interpersonal behavior; group dynamics; leadership and teamwork; organizational structure and design; decision-making; power; conflict; and negotiation.

And this represents just a selection. OB is a big subject which does not lend itself to a potted-history approach. Most guides to the topic are substantial – Buchanan and Huczynski's introductory text,[3] for example, weighs in at over 900 pages. Against this backdrop, what follows is an impressionistic cherry-pick of some key themes.

Henri Fayol and the first principles of management

The roots of modern-day organizations can be traced back at least 2000 years to models of Chinese military hierarchy. However, one of the first people to capture on paper the processes and practices of organizations was Henri Fayol (1841–1925), a mining engineer and manager by profession. Fayol defined the nature and working patterns of the twentieth-century organization in his book, *General and Industrial Management*, published in 1916. In it, he laid down what he called 14 principles of management.

HENRY FAYOL'S 14 PRINCIPLES OF MANAGEMENT

1 Division of work: tasks should be divided up with employees specializing in a limited set of tasks so that expertise is developed and productivity increased.

2 Authority and responsibility: authority is the right to give orders and entails enforcing them with rewards and penalties; authority should be matched with corresponding responsibility.

3 Discipline: this is essential for the smooth running of business and is dependent on good leadership, clear and fair arguments, and the judicious application of penalties.

4 Unity of command: for any action whatsoever, an employee should receive orders from one superior only; otherwise authority, discipline, order, and stability are threatened.

5 Unity of direction: a group of activities concerned with a single objective should be co-ordinated by a single plan under one head.

6 Subordination of individual interest to general interest: individual or group goals must not be allowed to override those of the business.

7 Remuneration of personnel: this may be achieved by various methods but it should be fair, encourage effort, and not lead to overpayment.

8 Centralization: the extent to which orders should be issued only from the top of the organization is a problem which should take into account its characteristics, such as size and the capabilities of the personnel.

9 Scalar chain (line of authority): communications should normally flow up and down the line of authority running from the top to the bottom of the organization, but sideways communication between those of equivalent rank in different departments can be desirable so long as superiors are kept informed.

10 Order: both materials and personnel must always be in their proper place; people must be suited to their posts so there must be careful organization of work and selection of personnel.

11 Equity: personnel must be treated with kindness and justice.
12 Stability of tenure of personnel: rapid turnover of personnel should be avoided because of the time required for the development of expertise.
13 Initiative: all employees should be encouraged to exercise initiative within limits imposed by the requirements of authority and discipline.
14 *Esprit de corps*: efforts must be made to promote harmony within the organization and prevent dissension and divisiveness.

The management function, Fayol believed, consisted of planning, organizing, commanding, co-ordinating and controlling. Many practicing managers, even today, would identify similar elements as the core of their activities.

Fayol was also one of the first people to characterize a commercial organization's activities into its basic components. He suggested that organizations could be sub-divided into six main areas of activity:

» technical
» commercial
» financial
» security
» accounting
» management.

In defining the core principles governing how organizations worked and the contribution of management to that process, Fayol in effect laid down a blueprint that has shaped organization thinking for a century.

Frederick Taylor and the school of scientific management

Frederick W. Taylor is often described as the world's first efficiency expert and "the father of scientific management." Although he lived through little of it – he died in 1915, aged 59 – Taylor's influence on the twentieth century is unquestionable. Peter Drucker, for example, rates him alongside Freud and Darwin as a maker of the modern world.

Taylor was one of the first to attempt to systematically analyze human behavior at work. He advocated the use of time-and-motion study as a means of standardizing work activities. His scientific approach called for detailed observation and measurement of even the most routine work, to find the optimum mode of performance.

The results were dramatic, with productivity increasing significantly. As time went by, new organizational functions like personnel and quality control were created. Of course, in breaking down each task to its smallest unit to find what Taylor called "the one best way" to do each job, the effect was to remove human variability. And so Taylor lay the ground for the mass production techniques that dominated management thinking in the first half of the twentieth century.

SCIENTIFIC MANAGEMENT: TAYLOR'S FIVE SIMPLE PRINCIPLES

1 Shift all responsibility for the organization of work from the worker to the manager; managers should do all the thinking relating to the planning and design of work, leaving the workers with the task of implementation.
2 Use scientific methods to determine the most efficient way of doing work; assign the worker's task accordingly, specifying the precise way in which the work is to be done.
3 Select the best person to perform the job thus designed.
4 Train the worker to do the work efficiently.
5 Monitor worker performance to ensure that appropriate work procedures are followed and that appropriate results are achieved.

The Human Relations Movement

Because the industrialists of the early decades of the twentieth century followed Taylor's lead and put the emphasis on efficiency, it was some years before any significant attention was paid to the needs and motivations of that other major factor involved in the work process – the workers. One of the early pioneers of a view that actually people were central to the world of business was Mary Parker Follett (1868–1933).

Although she has achieved an almost legendary status since her death, her views were largely ignored at the time by the business world.

Increasingly, though, during the 1930s, criticism of scientific management mounted. Elton Mayo was just one on those who thought Taylor's ideas were dehumanizing and alienating. Mayo was an integral part of the Human Relations Movement. Although not formally constituted, this Movement embodied the thinking of many who were concerned at the apparent disregard shown to workers by Taylor's one best way, and who felt that, actually, there was a better way – one which acknowledged people as capable of a much more creative contribution to the work process than Taylorism allowed, and one which set out to create a more open and trusting work environment.

HUMAN RELATIONS MOVEMENT: SOME OPERATING PRINCIPLES

1 Organizations are social – and not just economic – systems.
2 People are motivated by many needs, not just financial reward.
3 The informal work group is a major influence on the attitudes and performance of individual workers.
4 Job roles are more complex than job descriptions and time-and-motion studies would suggest.
5 There is no particular correlation between individual and organizational needs.
6 Job satisfaction will lead to higher job productivity and this is a more socially beneficial approach than worker coercion.
7 Managers need strong social skills, not just technical skills.

With these seeds sown by the theorists, an increasing number of practitioners began to come on board. A number of people setting up businesses in the 1930s – people like Bill Hewlett and Dave Packard of Hewlett Packard, for instance – began to realize that the nature of the relationship between a company and its workforce impacts explicitly on the quality of contribution that individuals make. Treat people with respect and bear their needs and interests in mind, and they typically make a better contribution. Treat them as production fodder, and they park their brains outside before walking through the gates of the company and into work.

The slow-growing realization on the part of some organizations that extracting the optimal performance out of people required a more subtle understanding of the human heart and mind inevitably led to the creation of companies with a very different look and feel from the efficiency-obsessed Taylorist companies against which they were a reaction. Not that Taylorism was vanquished – arguably it retains a strong presence to this day in phenomena like business process reengineering, and in places like a good number of call centers. But at least now there was an alternative.

1950 to the present day

To a great extent, the last 50 years have been about deepening our understanding of those two major schools of thought – Taylorism's efficiency-centric view of organizations versus the people-centric view of the Human Relations supporters.

There have, of course, been many significant contributions to thinking about organizational behavior over the years – Abraham Maslow on human behavior and motivation; Douglas McGregor's Theory X and Theory Y; Edgar Schein on culture; Meredith Belbin and others on teams; Peter Senge and others on learning; and so on (see the list of influential publications below). But the fundamental battle-lines drawn up in the first half of the twentieth century remain in place.

That said, there is now an emerging view that perhaps there may be a third way – one which combines the best elements of scientific management and human relations.

Quite what an organization embracing this third way would look like is up for conjecture. There is currently some quite interesting work going on in some call centers to bring a more human face to their efficiency-obsessed, Dickensian cultures. But at the time of writing, there is no obvious best-practice organization that has achieved this melding of approaches.

For now, the best way to characterize how much things have changed over the past century is to bring matters down to an individual level. Compare Henry Fayol's 14 principles of management (above) with the following list featured by Charles Leadbeater and Kate Oakley in their recent pamphlet called *The Independents: Britain's New Cultural Entrepreneurs.*[4]

HOW TO MAKE IT AS AN INDEPENDENT

1 Be prepared to have several goes. You're unlikely to make it first time around. Learn from failure, don't wallow in it.

2 Timing is critical. Technology is moving so fast it's easy to be either too early or too late.

3 Don't have a plan. It will come unstuck because it's too inflexible.

4 Have an intuition and a feel for where the market is headed. Adapt and change with the consumers.

5 Be brave enough to be distinctive. If you are doing what everyone else is doing, you're in the wrong business.

6 Be passionate. If you don't believe in what you are doing, nobody else will. At the outset only passion will persuade other people to back you.

7 Keep your business lean. Buy top-of-the-range computers but put them on second-hand desks. Necessity is the mother of invention, not luxury.

8 Make work fun. If it stops being fun, people will not be creative.

9 Give your employees a stake in the business. You may not be able to pay them much to start with so give them shares.

10 Pick partners who are as committed as you. To start with, a business will only be sustained by a band of believers.

11 Don't be sentimental. Be ready to split with your partners – often your best friends – when the business faces a crisis or a turning point.

12 Create products that can become ubiquitous quickly. For example, by creating something that can be given away in a global market, thereby attracting huge stock market valuations.

13 Don't aim to become the next Bill Gates. Aim to get bought out by him.

14 Take a holiday in Silicon Valley. You will be convinced anyone is capable of anything.

The contrast between the two is very marked, and the underlying assumptions about the nature of work even more so. Leadbeater and

Table 3.1 A brief history of organizational theory.

Speed of change	School of thought	Date
Relatively slow	Classical management theory (focused on planning, organizing, commanding employees, coordinating activities, and controlling performance; specialization of work)	1900 onwards
	Machine metaphor	
	Principles of management: Henri Fayol	
	Scientific management	
	Job design, time and motion: Frederick Taylor	
	Bureaucracy: Max Weber	
	Rational school of human behavior	
Stable	Human Relations school of management (focused on the importance of the attitudes and feelings of workers)	1930s to 1960s
	Organic metaphor	
	Hawthorne effect	
	Motivation theory (Maslow, Herzberg, etc.)	
	Importance of the working environment	
	Non rationality	
	Beginnings of leadership theory	

(Continued overleaf)

Table 3.1 (Continued).

Speed of change	School of thought	Date
Faster – increasingly unstable	Pick and mix theories Cultural metaphor (cultural web) Contingency theory Organizational life cycle Growing impact of technology Strategy and goals Matrix management	1960s to 1980s
Very rapid change – highly unstable	Organizations in transition Learning metaphor Technological transformation Boundaryless and virtual organizations Outsourcing Horizontal organizations Systems approach Personal mastery – Senge *et al.* Team-based organizations	Late 1980s onwards

Oakley may not be describing the world of work as we are all currently experiencing it, but they do articulate a mindset about work that couldn't be further away from Fayol's conception. There is no doubt about it: we've come a long way. Table 3.1 shows some of the major milestones.

LANDMARK PUBLICATIONS ON ORGANIZATIONAL BEHAVIOR

- » **1911**: Frederick Taylor: *Principles of Scientific Management*
- » **1916**: Henri Fayol: *General and Industrial Management*
- » **1924**: Max Weber: *The Theory of Social and Economic Organization*
- » **1933**: Elton Mayo: *Human Problems of an Industrial Civilization*
- » **1938**: Chester Barnard: *The Functions of the Executive*
- » **1954**: Abraham Maslow: *Motivation and Personality*
- » **1956**: William Whyte: *The Organization Man*
- » **1959**: Frederick Herzberg: *The Motivation to Work*
- » **1960**: Douglas McGregor: *The Human Side of Enterprise*
- » **1964**: Robert Blake and Jane Mouton: *The Managerial Grid*
- » **1973**: Henry Mintzberg: *The Nature of Managerial Work*
- » **1978**: Chris Argyris and Donald Schon: *Organizational Learning*
- » **1979**: Reg Revans: *Action Learning*
- » **1981**: Richard Pascale and Anthony Athos: *The Art of Japanese Management*
- » **1982**: Tom Peters and Bob Waterman: *In Search of Excellence*
- » **1984**: Meredith Belbin: *Management Teams*
- » **1985**: Edgar Schein: *Organizational Culture and Leadership*
- » **1986**: Gareth Morgan: *Images of Organization*
- » **1989**: Charles Handy: *The Age of Unreason*
- » **1990**: Peter Senge: *The Fifth Discipline*
- » **1990**: Richard Pascale: *Managing on the Edge*
- » **1993**: James Champy and Mike Hammer: *Re-engineering the Corporation*
- » **1994**: Jerry Porras and James Collins: *Built to Last*

- » **1995**: Karl Weick: *Sensemaking in Organizations*
- » **1997**: Arie de Geus: *The Living Company*
- » **1997**: Thomas Stewart: *Intellectual Capital*
- » **2000**: Richard Pascale: *Surfing the Edge of Chaos*
- » **2001**: Daniel Pink: *Free Agent Nation*

NOTES

1 Herzberg, F. (1968) *Work and the Nature of Man*, World Publishing, Cleveland, OH.
2 Quinn Mills, D. (1991) *Rebirth of the Corporation*, Wiley, New York.
3 Buchanan, D. & Huczynski, A. (2001) *Organizational Behavior: An Introductory Text*, 4th edn, FT/Prentice Hall, Harlow.
4 Leadbeater, C. & Oakley, K. (1999) *The Independents: Britain's New Cultural Entrepreneurs*, Demos, London.

The E-Dimension

» How the Internet is changing our thinking about various aspects of organizational life, including hierarchy, decision-making, internal communication, the working day, and knowledge management.
» How well are we coping with technological change?

"The twenty-first century will not be a dark age. Neither will it deliver to most people the bounties promised by the most extraordinary technological revolution in history. Rather, it may well be characterized by informed bewilderment."[1]

Manuel Castells

INTRODUCTION

To note that information technology is having an impact on organizations is on a par with saying that Madonna seems to notch up the occasional column inch. Despite those gainsayers who have noted the demise of innumerable dot-coms with a degree of malicious glee, the fact is that the impact of the Internet and allied technologies has already been significant and can only increase over the coming years.

However, when it comes to assessing that impact, we hit a small problem. There's a well known aphorism that if you want to find out about water, then don't go asking a fish. Just as water quickly becomes unremarkable when you spend all your time swimming in it, so we humans have a remarkable capacity for accommodating technological change with barely a second glance.

And yet all the major technologies have significant, if subtle, impacts on the way we work and live. Take the lightbulb. Before the invention of the electric light by Thomas Edison, people used to sleep an average of 10 hours a night. These days, we sleep on average for just over seven hours, with one-third of people getting by on less than six hours.[2] More recently, the mobile phone has gone from being the stuff of futuristic science programs to commonplace in a handful of years.

In terms of extent and speed of impact, though, the Internet has outpaced all of the great disruptive technologies of the twentieth century – electricity, the telephone, the motor car, and so on. Amid everything else it is doing, the Internet is re-inventing the nature of work.

There are plenty of people writing about the impact of technology at a high level. There is no doubt that technology has enabled the creation of a global marketplace. Books and articles abound on "the death of distance",[3] "the conquest of location",[4] the irrelevance of size, the subjugation of time, and so on.

THE INTERNET AND ORGANIZATIONS

"Corporate life spans are shrinking. Remember a little outfit called Netscape? Netscape was formed in 1994, went public in 1995, and was gone by 1999, subsumed into AOL's operation. This giant of the new economy reached only its fourth birthday. Question: Was Netscape a company – or was it really an extremely cool project? More important question: Does the distinction matter?"

"Here's what does matter: That short-lived entity put several products on the market, prompted powerful companies (notably Microsoft) to shift strategies, and equipped a few thousand individuals with experience, wealth, and connections that they could bring to their next project."

"The lesson: People, not companies, are 'built to last.' Most of us will outlive any organization for which we work."[5]

Daniel Pink

In terms of our day-to-day experience, here are just some of the ways in which the Internet is changing the fabric of our working lives.

Internet start-ups carry little or no organizational baggage

There are very few chief executives of more traditional, bricks-and-mortar companies who would admit to being totally happy with the structure, shape, and size of their organizations.

Also it seems that most CEOs are less than enamoured of the people that work for them and alongside them. A survey carried out in 1999 by the Institute of Directors and Development Dimensions International asked senior directors what percentage of their employees they would rehire if they could change all their employees overnight. Some 50% said they would rehire between zero and 40%. Only 7%, moreover, expressed confidence in the leadership capabilities of their peers within their organizations.

Internet start-ups do not face these problems, at least not in the early days. The organization is consciously designed and the people involved are hand-picked. They do not, in short, suffer from what a CEO client of mine calls "inherited incompetence."

Hierarchy

A traditional organization is structured around two key concepts – the breakdown and management of goals and tasks through the use of hierarchy and stable employee relationships over prolonged periods of time. In Internet organizations, structures are more flexible and dynamic. Hierarchy has not vanished but it has been augmented by distributed lattices of interconnections.

In an interview on *The Motley Fool Radio Show* in April 2000, CEO Tim Koogle described the set-up at Yahoo!: "It's not hierarchical. We do have a structure in the company because you need a structure to have some order on things, but it's a pretty flat organization."

For well-established organizations, Shoshana Zuboff of Harvard Business School believes that a rigid hierarchy gets in the way of making best use of technology. She writes:

"The successful reinvention of the firm consistent with the demands of an information economy will continue to be tragically limited as long as the principal features of modern work are preserved. Unlocking the promise of an information economy now depends on dismantling the very same managerial hierarchy that once brought greatness."[6]

Decision-making

In an e-business, as with more traditional businesses, the leadership team typically make all the big strategic decisions about what the company is going to do. The difference is that decision-making in e-businesses is often a more collaborative process. At Yahoo! for example, Tim Koogle has described how working in adjoining cubicles affects the leadership team's approach to decision-making: "During a normal day, you'll find us hollering back and forth across the wall, bouncing around inside the cubes, grabbing each other and going off into a little conference room."

Another facet of decision-making in Internet start-ups is that companies grow too fast to be managed closely from the center. Decisions, once taken centrally, are rapidly devolved to those working in the business to determine the method and manner of implementation.

Internal communication

This is not a problem for e-businesses in the early days when the organization consists of a small group of highly motivated people who spend a lot of time in each other's company, and who therefore automatically keep themselves and each other in the picture. However, business growth needs to be fuelled by new blood. By definition these are people who were not part of the original setup and therefore processes and systems need to be introduced to ensure that everybody is kept informed – it no longer happens naturally.

For Internet businesses, the speed of growth means that the need for more formalized communication systems can kick in very quickly. The ill-fated boo.com, for example, went from 12 or so people to over 400 in less than a year.

The working day now lasts 24 hours

Information technology has the capacity not only to change where knowledge and power reside in the organization; it also changes time. The "working day" has less meaning in a global village where communication via e-mail, voicemail, and facsimile transmissions can be sent or received at any time of day or night. Paradoxically, as the working day has expanded, so time has contracted. Companies compete on speed, using effective co-ordination of resources to reduce the time needed to develop new products, deliver orders or react to customer requests.

> "People are now becoming the most expensive optional component of the productive process and technology is becoming the cheapest."[7]
>
> *Michael Dunkerley*

Growth has been decoupled from employment

Particularly during the 1980s, it became more and more apparent that the real bottom line of technology was that it made jobs go away. It didn't happen all at once. But, starting in the manufacturing industries and then moving into white-collar work, every day more work was being automated. And both the white-collar workplace and the factory floor were transformed.

Not enough good people to go around

For most e-businesses, the factor that limits or enables rapid growth is their capacity to recruit and retain good people. Finding the right people to sustain rapid growth is problematic for any business at any stage of its life cycle. For an unproven e-business start-up, particularly now that the Internet economy has lost its luster, it can be virtually impossible. Significantly, most of the consultancy fees paid by e-business start-ups to date have gone to specialist recruitment companies.

The workplace becomes transparent

Shoshana Zuboff argues, in an article for *Scientific American*,[8] that information technologies transform work at every organizational level by potentially giving all employees a comprehensive or near-comprehensive view of the entire business. These technologies surrender knowledge to anyone with the requisite skills. This contrasts with earlier generations of technological advance, where the primary impact of new machines was to decrease the complexity of tasks.

Technology also facilitates the open sharing of know-how within a company. By and large, e-businesses have a better track record at knowledge management. Many traditional companies retain a "knowledge is power" mentality, and even those that consciously set out to create a knowledge-sharing environment can fall foul of knowledge-hoarding by suspicious business units or individuals fearful of becoming dispensable.

The rise of the virtual organization

Virtual organizations are formed by a cluster of interested parties to achieve a specific aim – perhaps to bring a specific product or idea to market – and then disappear when the aim has been achieved. The concept is not just a useful tactic for corporate downsizing, it also carries ideological weight. Manuel Castells argues that:

> "it is not accidental that the metaphor – virtual – is cybernetic, for the information highway facilitates a loose corporate web connected by modem rather than physical affinity or long-term relationship. The worker brings to the marketplace only his human

capital. The virtual corporation pays only for the value the worker can add. If the worker gets weary of the insecurity, the solution is obvious. He should become an entrepreneur himself. We are all Bill Gates – or at least we should be."[9]

Working from home

It is technically possible for a worker to be based at home using e-mail and other technology to communicate with colleagues and the outside world generally. In reality, this isn't what most people want from work. It is significant that even the high-tech pioneers tend to cluster in hotspots like Silicon Valley to enable them to talk with and learn from like-minded others.

THE IMPACT OF TECHNOLOGY – A FINAL THOUGHT

The introduction to this chapter discussed the remarkable capacity we have to absorb new technologies like the mobile phone. And it's probably true – we can cope with singular new technologies which augment a previous technology by adding a new feature – e.g. from fixed base phones to mobiles. But the Internet's impact on working life is different. It doesn't just augment, it transforms our experience of work. It transforms where we work, how we work, when we work – even *whether* we work. The job for life has disappeared, never to return. Working life has never felt so insecure for so many.

The electronic digital frontier is beckoning. In the final analysis, the issue is not the capacity of the technology, it's our capacity to cope. Shoshana Zuboff certainly believes that the technological tail is wagging the human dog. In just 15 words from her book *In the Age of the Smart Machine* – a book all the more remarkable for being written back in the 1980s – Zuboff sums up the challenge we now face. "So far," she writes, "patterns of morality, sociality, and feeling are evolving much more slowly than technology."

THE RISE OF THE CYBER COTTAGE INDUSTRY

In recent years, Tom Peters, co-author of *In Search of Excellence* and probably the world's best known management guru, has been looking at how changes at a corporate, national, and global level impact on the nature of work for us as individuals. It is a topical theme that takes a variety of guises – knowledge workers making a living out of Charles Leadbeater's "thin air;" McKinsey warning its clients that the biggest challenge for companies is "the war for talent;" Tom Peters' "brand called you;" Harriet Rubin's "soloists;" business magazines like *Fast Company* devoted to Me Inc. or me.com and full of advice on "why it pays to quit," how you should be hot-desking with colleagues, telecommuting from home, and generally reconsidering your whole future.

Charles Handy paints this picture of the twenty-first century world of work:

> "It's obviously going to be a different kind of world ... It will be a world of fleas and elephants, of large conglomerates and small individual entities, of large political and economic blocs and small countries. The smart thing is to be the flea on the back of the elephant. Think of Ireland and the EU, or consultants and the BBC. A flea can be global as easily as one of the elephants but can more easily be swept away. Elephants are a guarantee of continuity but fleas provide the innovation. There will also be ad hoc organizations, temporary alliances of fleas and elephants to deliver a particular project."[10]

The Internet gives added impetus to anybody considering the "flea" life, either totally on their own or with a cluster of like minds. In *The Death of Distance*,[11] Frances Cairncross describes how, by using technology creatively, small companies can now offer services that, in the past, only giants could provide. What's more, the cost of starting new businesses is declining, and so more small companies will spring up. Many companies will become networks of independent specialists; more employees will therefore work in smaller units or alone.

Individuals with valuable ideas can attract global venture capital. Perhaps one of the most telling features of the new economy is that increasing numbers of people can describe themselves without irony as one-person global companies.

NOTES

1 Castells, M. (1998) *The Information Economy*, Blackwell, Cambridge, MA.
2 Research by Cornell University as reported in *The Guardian*, 9 September 1997.
3 Cairncross, F. (1997) *The Death of Distance*, Orion, London.
4 Micklethwait, J. & Wooldridge, A. (2000) *A Future Perfect*, Heinemann, London.
5 Pink, D. (2001) "Land of the free," *Fast Company* **46**, p.125. (www.fastcompany.com/online/46/freeagent.html)
6 Zuboff, S. (1988) *In the Age of the Smart Machine: The Future of Work and Power*, Basic Books, New York.
7 Dunkerley, M. (1996) *The Jobless Economy*, Polity, Cambridge.
8 Zuboff, S. (1995) "The emperor's new workplace," *Scientific American,* September, p.164.
9 Castells, *op. cit.*
10 Handy, C. (1999) in *CBI News*, October. (From text of speech given by Handy at the CBI National Conference '99.)
11 Cairncross, *op. cit.*

The Global Dimension

» The stages involved in becoming a global player.
» Six key principles that underpin effective management on a global scale.
» The implications of globalization for individuals.
» Case study: Tesco.

"Globalization is not the only reason for . . . uncertainty, but, with the possible exception of technological innovation, it is the main destabilizer of the management psyche."[1]

John Micklethwait and Adrian Wooldridge

When Nissan established a car plant at Sunderland, hailed at the time as a new lease of life for the moribund British car industry, the Japanese company commissioned a television PR campaign. In the advertisement, a northern worker expresses satisfaction at Nissan's arrival in an unintelligible English dialect, which is "translated" for the viewer's benefit by a smartly dressed, precisely spoken Japanese businessman. The advertisement was very funny, but locally (in the north east) people complained so much that it had to be taken off the air.

Although Nissan has since gone on to make a tremendous success of their Sunderland plant, with workers successfully adopting many Japanese-based quality practices, the story is nonetheless one of the more eye-catching indicators that the corporate road to globalization is fraught with pitfalls.

WHAT IS GLOBALIZATION?

Globalization is an economic process, the result of human innovation and technological progress. It refers to the increasing integration of economies around the world, particularly through trade and financial flows. The term sometimes also refers to the movement of people (labor) and knowledge (technology) across international borders.

In their brilliant book *A Future Perfect*, John Micklethwait and Adrian Wooldridge, both journalists for the *Economist*, argue that there are four stages to becoming a truly global company:

1 *Corporate colonialism*: using foreign outposts simply as "dumb terminals" to distribute domestic goods.
2 *Cheap hands*: using foreign labor because it cost less than domestic workers.

3 *Going transnational*: companies begin to use their foreign subsidiaries for ideas as well as implementation, and to tailor global products for local markets.

4 *Genuinely multicultural multinationals*: nationality of company employees ceases to matter. The best global companies take the best skills and ideas from wherever they are in the world. Global management has to be multicultural. This stage is less to do with structure than attitude of mind.

Micklethwait and Wooldridge go on to outline the six principles that they believe need to underpin a company's effort to become an international player.

THE SIX PRINCIPLES OF GLOBAL MANAGEMENT

1 *Management matters, particularly when it comes to corporate culture.* The ability of the top management team to deliver top quality at a competitive cost becomes paramount when competing in the global marketplace. In 1998, General Motors spent twice as much on labor per car produced as Toyota; a good part of that differential was due to the fact that GM was simply less efficient than its rival, and that in turn is a management responsibility.

2 *Size complicates.* According to research by the London Business School, around 50% of the companies that operate internationally employ fewer than 250 employees. Technology-enabled small companies can offer services that, in the past, only giants had the scale and scope to provide. Just as Microsoft could appear from virtually nowhere to usurp the market of mighty IBM, so a few years later Netscape appeared overnight and threatened to undermine the market (and the size) of Microsoft. Who will be next? And where will they come from? In this globalized world, small agile companies have an advantage over giant organizations that are unable to take decisions quickly. On the other hand, while small companies find it easier to reach markets around the world, big companies will more readily offer high-quality local services, such as putting customers

in one part of the world directly in touch with expertise in other places, and monitoring more precisely the quality of local provision.

3 *The things that define good national management also define good international management.* As Sony's financially disastrous excursion to Hollywood showed, even the best companies can leave their brains at home. It was only the installation of a new manager operating good management practices that turned Sony's 1995 loss of $1.7bn into a profit of $3.4bn in 1997.

4 *It pays to behave ethically.* Some multinationals have treated their overseas operations a bit like a "lads' holiday" where all normal rules of good behavior are suspended. However, in a world where reputation is becoming an ever more prized asset, it makes good business sense for a company to play to its genuine strengths rather than cynically exploit its host country's weaknesses.

5 *Global management is about how well companies husband human capital, knowledge in particular.* There is a tendency for companies to think that their home talent is best; these companies deny themselves access to the full global pool of talent at their disposal. Companies will happily talk about ambitions for a significant proportion of business profits to come from overseas but seem less willing to recruit the same proportion of top managers from overseas. This is the culture dilemma: bring forward local talent, and become more multicultural; while on the other hand remaining loyal to the culture that brought you national success in the first place.

6 *Far from dissipating the effect of personality, globalization has made leadership even more important.* Company leaders who operate on a global platform find that both their strengths and weaknesses are amplified. Also, just as a successful manager of a club football team needs a different skill set to succeed as a national coach, so global leaders need to recognize that there may also be additional skills needed to be effective in a particular country's work environment.

GLOBALIZATION: MORE THAN JUST AN MBA LECTURE TOPIC

There was a time when globalization was only a concern for multinational companies and business studies students. But the fact is there are plenty of ways in which globalization can impact on your organization, no matter what its size or industry sector. Which of the following might apply to you or your company?

» Sources of competition: your biggest competitor could now be anywhere in the world.

» Manufacturing capacity will continue to shift from western economies to those countries with access to cheaper labor. Equally, technology is allowing more and more knowledge-based work to be shipped to the cheapest environment. This may bring jobs to emerging economies but can create severe pressures for unskilled workers in more advanced economies.

» Traditional jobs still exist – but not here. As Kevin Kelly has put it, "the old economies will continue to operate profitably within the deep cortex of the new economy."[2] The fact is that around the world there are just as many cars and ships being constructed as ever, just as many roads being built, just as much coal being produced, as much steel being made. The difference is where they are now being produced. "Traditional" industries are all thriving elsewhere in the world.

» In a world of instant communication, it's harder to sustain a lead in innovation. Product improvements can rapidly get copied.

» We are also seeing the internationalization of business practices, with techniques like business process re-engineering now being deployed globally.

» A key challenge for companies will be to hire and retain good people, extracting value from them, rather than allowing them to keep all the value they create for themselves. A company will constantly need to convince its best employees that working for it enhances each individual's value.

» With the relentless if rocky rise of the World Wide Web (and don't forget that it *is* worldwide), new channels of distribution, and entirely new business models, are being created faster than ever before. All the traditional assumptions that business leaders may have learned at business school – about strategy, pricing, selling, how to manage people, and so on – are under fierce attack. The Web has the capacity to turn every company in every industry upside down and inside out.

» Culture and communications networks, rather than rigid management structures, will hold companies together. Many companies will become networks of independent specialists; more employees will therefore work in smaller units or alone.

» As the workforce becomes ever more diverse, cultural awareness training becomes not merely a token nod in the direction of political correctness, but a crucial part of enhancing both managerial and front-line effectiveness.

» Geography is becoming less important and people are becoming more mobile. A new breed of graduate and post-graduate is emerging that has the confidence to look beyond national boundaries to the international job market. Within organizations, we are seeing a workforce that grows increasingly transient, and that is prepared to move between companies and even continents.

The bottom line is that the world of work has changed irrevocably. The collective impact of globalization and technology is that none of us any longer has a protected, inviolable career. If there is a cheaper or better quality alternative to you and your skill set anywhere in the world, you are at risk. Darwin was right: if you can't outpace your environment, you're doomed.

CASE STUDY: TESCO – A GLOBAL SHOP FOR GLOBAL PEOPLE

Succeeding in the international retail sector is no mean feat. In recent times, Marks and Spencer confidently expanded their business overseas, only to return chastised to base a few years later with heavy financial losses and its reputation badly dented.

Tesco is that real rarity – a UK retailer that is proving it can thrive on an international stage. If all goes to plan, Tesco should break through the £1bn profit barrier for the second year running in 2001. Although we British tend to think of Tesco as a grocer, it has in recent times expanded into non-food areas like clothes, books, electrical appliances, and DVDs. And with some success – the company now accounts for 4% of the UK non-food market.

Although Tesco seems like quite a traditional retailer – walk into the company's head office in Cheshunt and the impression is of an organization that hasn't changed much in 30 years – it avoided the pitfall of corporate colonialism that all too many UK companies have succumbed to. It didn't, in other words, simply try to export and impose the practices that have worked so well in the UK.

CEO Terry Leahy quickly embraced the concept that each country in which Tesco intended to stake a place in would require a different approach – one that was acclimatized to the indigenous culture. "Once you make that break," he said in an interview, "it helps in a lot of little ways. You don't make subsequent mistakes."[3]

This means that the stores themselves often look different to the UK model. They are also normally run by natives of the country. In France, for example, Carrefour's stores are run by French managers. The advantage of this, says Leahy is that "instinctively, the store is local, in the way it merchandises and promotes its goods, or selects its product according to local tastes, seasons or events." To achieve this level of understanding, Tesco sends a team into a country long enough to understand the politics, the culture, and the competition.

What underpins Tesco's success, both nationally and internationally, in Leahy's view is that the company "never had an office class. There was no special graduate scheme; you can start anywhere in the business and you get on according to your own ability." In other words, Tesco will let people go as far as their skills will take them.

Tesco's approach may be meritocratic but it certainly isn't *laissez faire*. Management development is a key instrument for the company. That, and working hard at imbuing a set of values about how the company deals with customers, staff, and suppliers.

Leahy believes that the Tesco formula for success is straightforward. "Tesco has three skills," he says. "How we understand customers. How we manage people. How we use technology."

NOTES

1 Micklethwait, J. & Wooldridge, A. (2000) *A Future Perfect*, Heinemann, London.
2 Kelly, K. (1998) *New Rules for the New Economy*, Fourth Estate, London, p.7.
3 Leahy, T. (2001) quoted in "One step ahead," *Business Voice*, November.

The State of the Art

» The knowledge dilemma – to share or to hoard?
» Organizations – does Darwin rule?
» Attitudes to work.
» The power of language.
» Women, men, work and home.
» The war for talent.
» The end of careers.

"It has become professionally legitimate in the United States to accept and utilize ideas without an in-depth grasp of their underlying foundation, and without the commitment necessary to sustain them."[1]

Richard Pascale

"Learning is the new form of labor. [It is] no longer a separate activity that occurs either before one enters the workplace or in remote classroom settings . . . Learning is at the heart of productive activity."[2]

Shoshana Zuboff

"Chance favors the prepared mind"

Louis Pasteur

Nineteenth-century scientist Pasteur believed that somebody who has gone to the trouble of obtaining relevant knowledge, skills, and understanding in a given area is more likely come up with valuable insights than somebody else who has given the subject little or no thought.

On that basis, understanding the key issues in the field of organizational behavior does not guarantee that you will create a new theory or even manage future challenges more effectively than the next person, but the chances are that you will.

That said, trying to predict what the future world of work will hold for us all seems like a doomed pastime. It wasn't all that long ago that a technology-enriched future was going to bring prosperity for all, and with it, less hours at work, not to mention a life of leisure. Instead, we in the UK now work the longest hours in Europe, and a life of leisure funded by being paid more for doing less seems like a pipedream.

One thing is certain: when it comes to the twenty-first century world of work, impermanence is in and jobs-for-life are out. As the writer Naomi Klein puts it in her book *No Logo*:[3]

"Offering employment – the steady kind, with benefits, holiday pay, a measure of security and maybe even union representation – has fallen out of economic fashion."

It's difficult to imagine a scenario in which jobs-for-life could make anything like a meaningful comeback. Companies lose money – and they purge staff. Companies announce record profits – and they purge staff. The correlation between company profit and job growth, according to Klein, has never been weaker.

Against this highly uncertain backdrop, the business airwaves are abuzz with books, articles, conferences, and videos exhorting the modern manager to take on board the latest big ideas: the application of complexity theory to business; lessons behind the rise and fall of the dot-coms; the ripped up psychological contract between organization and individual; the balanced scorecard; managing in a downturn; the end of loyalty; the return of loyalty; emotional intelligence; the narcissistic leader; the smart organization; the free agent nation; and so on.

This chapter explores a handful of the emergent ideas and concepts that are clamoring for managerial attention. Some will certainly prove to be substantive; others may be cul-de-sacs. Some will apply at the macro level, others may strike at the very heart of your experience of work. All will hopefully provoke your thinking. Reflect, discuss, and beyond that, trust your judgment.

These are the key ideas covered in this section:

» the knowledge dilemma – to share or to hoard?
» organizations – does Darwin rule?
» attitudes to work;
» the power of language;
» agescape: demographics and the workplace;
» women, men, work, and home;
» interlude – the way we work;
» the war for talent;
» the end of careers 1; and
» the end of careers 2.

In addition, scattered around this section you will find a number of "zeitbites" – short, provocative quotes or snippets of information that help to capture the spirit of our current organizational age.

THE KNOWLEDGE DILEMMA – TO SHARE OR TO HOARD?

There are many who argue that knowledge management or intellectual capital will be the foundation of corporate success over the coming decade. If companies are set to stand or fall by their management of their intellectual capital (defined by Thomas Stewart, an early writer on the topic as "packaged useful knowledge"), then their ability to develop appropriate systems and to provide a setting within which people will be willing to share their knowledge becomes a crucial organizational challenge.

And yet according to a study led by Adrian Patch, a research psychologist for Birkbeck College in London, workers have responded to the end of the job-for-life culture by becoming "professional parasites," hoarding their expertise in the fear that sharing knowledge makes them more dispensable. One in five workers thought it was not in his or her interest to share knowledge at work, costing business billions of pounds a year in missed business opportunities, inefficient systems, and training.

The study uncovered tensions between companies who have put in computer infrastructures to enable the sharing of knowledge and information, and the willingness of employees to do so. The study found that if employees want to impress a potential permanent employer, they are as likely to share information and seek to build a good reputation as contented staff employees. However, those who feel threatened or unappreciated at work guard their niche knowledge jealously, making effective teamwork – which depends on the open exchange of information – virtually impossible. Companies who encourage employees to manage their own careers but who at the same time create dissatisfaction by failing to fulfil their promises risk losing important knowledge that is often a key part of the company's value.

ZEITBITE

"It's obviously going to be a different kind of world in the next century ... It will be a world of fleas and elephants, of large conglomerates and small individual entities, of large political and economic blocs and small countries. The smart thing is to be the flea on the back of the elephant. Think of Ireland and the EU, or consultants and the BBC."

"A flea can be global as easily as one of the elephants but can more easily be swept away. Elephants are a guarantee

of continuity but fleas provide the innovation. There will
also be ad hoc organizations, temporary alliances of fleas and
elephants to deliver a particular project."[4]

Charles Handy

ORGANIZATIONS – DOES DARWIN RULE?

"For the more conventional organization of modern times, we
encounter the contradictions so masterfully satirized by the Dilbert
cartoon strip – employees who are cynical about employment and
mistrustful of de-layering because they recognize that traditional
power and hidden hierarchy are alive and well and in control of
their destinies. The Dilbert characters seem to know what any
evolutionary psychologist would tell you: hierarchy is forever."[5]

Nigel Nicholson

Over the past few years, the new science of evolutionary psychology –
called Modern Darwinism by some because it has its root in the theory
of natural selection – has been provoking widespread support and
criticism.

In essence, evolutionary psychology takes the view that people
today – no matter whether they are captains of industry or burger
flippers – pretty much retain the mentality of our Stone Age ancestors.
Nigel Nicholson, a professor of organizational behavior at London
Business School, has suggested that we are "hard wired" for certain
attitudes and behaviors.

In his book *Managing the Human Animal*,[6] Nicholson explores the
implications of this for managers. Below are some examples.

» *Communication*: According to Nicholson, our Stone Age ancestors
needed to exchange information in order to survive the unpredictable
conditions of the Savannah Plain. Thus, over time, the propensity to
gossip became part of our mental programming. Companies that try
to eradicate gossip at work might just as well try to change their
employees' favorite color or musical tastes. The lesson for managers
is that the "grapevine" performs a function that people value at

a deeply engrained level. It's more productive to put managerial energy into making sure that the "grapevine" contains the right information rather than try to eradicate it altogether.

» *Team size*: Evolutionary psychology explores the dynamics of the human group. Our ancestors' clans on the Savannah Plain, for example, appear to have had no more than 150 members. The message for managers is that people will likely be most effective in small organizational units.

» *Gender bias*: Most businesses, says Nicholson, are run to satisfy distinctively masculine drives: "Many businesses make few allowances for women, and those who want to succeed are reluctant to press for concessions for fear of being stigmatized as taking advantage of their gender." The organizational model is male, in the sense that it is based upon features that predominate more in male than in female psychology: technical focus, single-mindedness, competitiveness, and a desire for control and hierarchy.

ZEITBITE

Many senior managers still see themselves as a breed apart. A study of status and perks reveals that:

» in 17% of firms, managers have separate dining facilities;
» 38% of managers benefit from health insurance schemes not available to the wider workforce;
» 29% have longer holidays than their staff;
» 23% have separate toilet and/or shower facilities; and
» 33% still expect to be addressed as "Sir" or by their title.

Survey by the Manufacturing, Science and Finance Union, July 1997

In another book, *Territorial Games*,[7] author Annette Simmons explores organizational turf wars – why they occur and what we can do about them. Simmons identifies and describes ten different territorial games that are enacted within organizations.

1 *Occupation*: marking territory; monopolizing resources, relationships or information.

2 *Information manipulation*: withholding, covering up, or giving false information.

3 *Intimidation*: yelling, staring someone down, making threats (veiled or overt).

4 *Powerful alliances*: using relationships with powerful people to intimidate; name dropping.

5 *Invisible wall*: discreetly creating perceptions that undermine previous agreements.

6 *Strategic non-compliance*: agreeing to take action with no intention of acting.

7 *Discredit*: using personal attacks to undermine the reputation or credibility of others.

8 *Shun*: personally excluding an individual; influencing a group to treat another as an outsider.

9 *Camouflage*: creating distractions; deliberately triggering anxiety in others.

10 *Filibuster*: using excessive verbiage to prevent action; wearing others down by out-talking them.

These turf war tactics can be traced backed to their Darwinian roots. We are by instinct a territorial race, and turf wars have become the organizationally accepted alternative to fisticuffs.

In his book, Nicholson makes seven predictions about the future of organizations, based on the principles of evolutionary psychology.

1 We can adapt quite well to a semi-itinerant, mobile lifestyle, although it's not normal for our culture, so most people will still seek more traditional forms of employment.

2 The traditional idea of the career is a modern invention to fit the linear hierarchy of organizations and occupations. However, if these hierarchies disappeared, people would not have enough to aspire to.

3 The separating boundary between work and home is also an artifice of recent times. People's work will become more integrated with home, but while the prospect of the two being interlinked still exists, so will the office.

4 So-called virtual organizations may grow but people will still desire and create networks like clans and seek to find real community through working relationships.

5 People will always want to make and have things. We can't have virtual water or food – by the same token, there will never be no work or jobs to do.
6 People will always desire face-to-face dealings.
7 People will always want to congregate in common spaces.

Writers on evolutionary psychology like Nicholson don't advocate that we return to a Stone Age way of life, rather that we need to try to understand how human nature and our hardwired sense of what behaviors are appropriate impacts on the way we live and work in the twenty-first century.

ZEITBITE

In these de-layered times, the concept of hierarchy has had a bad press. Here – with tongue partially, but only partially, in cheek – are ten reasons why "tall is beautiful."

1 Tall organizations reflect the nature of human society.
2 They recognize differences in human abilities.
3 They recognize the motivational value of upward progression.
4 They create an internal labor market and stimulate competition.
5 Natural spans of control force organizations to grow upwards and increasing complexity of technology and business limits the natural span of control.
6 Flatter structures force people to work too long to the detriment of family life.
7 New IT techniques reduce the dysfunctional features of steep hierarchies.
8 Organizational hierarchies exist the way they do because they match the psychological, sociological, anthropological, and economic needs of human beings.
9 All human societies are structured with differing levels of power and authority.
10 Organizations, including the earliest (armies, religions), fall into this pattern because it is natural for human beings to create and replicate such structures.

ATTITUDES TO WORK

A recent survey into attitudes to work found that, more than anything else, people would like to reduce the number of hours they spend working. The survey's full "top ten" list of desires that people expressed about work was as follows:[8]

1 Being able to work fewer hours
2 A change in the company culture
3 Work flexible hours
4 Reduce commuting – or avoid it
5 Work from home
6 Change jobs or relocate
7 More staff
8 Earn more
9 Retire
10 Reduce stress.

The survey also explored what people felt they had sacrificed in order to work. "Missing the children growing up" came top of the pile, followed by "work put before home and family," "moving home for employer," "missed leisure/hobby time," and "being away from home short-term."

The overriding sense one gets from this survey is that the working population laments the extent to which work life imposes on home life. And yet relatively few of us have actively sought to redress that balance; it often takes a forced change of circumstances, e.g. redundancy, to bring about a significant change. More often than not, our careers seem to manage us, rather than the other way round.

THE POWER OF LANGUAGE

In her book *Team Talk*,[9] Anne Donnellon of Harvard Business School uses anthropological and linguistic research techniques to focus on talk as the "medium through which team work is done and through which organizational and individual forces can be observed and analyzed." Given that language exchange is the primary way in which people swap information, make decisions, and formulate plans, Donnellon's book represents the long overdue entry of socio-linguistics into the field of management studies.

She looks at a team's use of language through six dimensions.

1 *Identification*: e.g. the use of terms like "we" or "us" to describe the team.
2 *Interdependence*: e.g. explicit references to independence or interdependence.
3 *Power differentiation*: e.g. challenges, corrections, verbal aggression, apologies.
4 *Social distance*: e.g. formal forms of address (Mr Blair or Tony), use of slang, nicknames.
5 *Conflict management tactics*: e.g. use of confrontational, accommodating, or avoidance language.
6 *Negotiation process*: e.g. use of win-win and win-lose language.

What emerges clearly from Donnellon's work is a sense of the significant extent to which the language used by teams both reflects and indeed shapes relationships within and outside the team.

AGESCAPE: DEMOGRAPHICS AND THE WORKPLACE[10]

Throughout history, societies have been extraordinarily young, with an average age of around 20. Within our lifetime, we will see that average rise to 50 in the West. Not only will the age balance shift, but populations in many countries are set to decline. In the late 1990s Japan became the first country ever with an average age of 40; in 2007 its population will reach a peak and then start falling. Italy will follow soon after, and by 2025 there will be more Italians aged over 50 than under that age. Populations in Europe are poised to plunge on a scale not seen since the Black Death in 1348.

The demographic changes will have an impact globally. They will also have an impact on some key area relevant to organizational life.

» The future *can* be viewed optimistically with the weight of numbers battering down ageism in the workplace and allowing people to work longer and more flexibly. However, if anything, the smaller numbers of young people available for work will start bidding wars for their services – scarcity, not glut, confers power in markets.

» The waves of downsizing and down-layering from the 1990s are likely to continue as companies shake out a perceived excess of middle-aged managers. The opportunities for many older workers will lie as subcontractors to large companies, whether as individual freelancers or by setting up their own small businesses.

» State pensions stand in the demographic firing line; in many countries pension promises are unaffordable and will have to be broken. The alternative is a quite unacceptable escalation in contributions, over-burdening the much smaller working population that will have to find the resources to honor these promises.

» All countries in the West will find their weight in the world diminishing. Favorable demographics will foster fast progress in developing countries, while many western countries will be hit by declining labor forces.

ZEITBITE

"I believe that 90% of white-collar jobs in the US will either be destroyed or altered beyond recognition in the next 10 to 15 years. That's a catastrophic prediction, given that 90% of us are engaged in white-collar work of one sort or another."[11]

Tom Peters

WOMEN, MEN, WORK, AND HOME[12]

Arlie Russell Hochschild, a sociology professor at the University of California, Berkeley, spent three years interviewing hundreds of employees of a Fortune 500 company renowned for its family-friendly policies, to see how they reconciled their work and their home life.

Where both parents worked – the norm other than for the company's most senior executives – a typical day would involve dropping the children off at the company's subsidized day-care center. The parents then spend a long – typically 10-hour – day at work before collecting their children from the center, doing the shopping, feeding everybody, washing the laundry, clearing up, putting the children to bed, and then heading to bed themselves, utterly exhausted. And these were the days when everything went according to plan.

Hochschild found that these parents rarely made use of the family-friendly policies promoted by the company. Rather they spent ever longer hours at work, regularly putting in significant bouts of overtime. In some cases, they needed the money. Often, however, both men and women, when faced with a choice between stress at work and stress at home, chose to work where at least they had contact with colleagues, were taken seriously, and got paid for their efforts. This contrasted with their home life where they felt isolated, taken for granted, and ground down by never-ending demands.

In *The Time Bind*,[13] a book based on her research, Hochschild offers the startling observation that for many work had become home, and home had become hard work. Perverse though the idea might seem, the book has clearly struck a chord, rapidly becoming a best-seller in the US.

ZEITBITE

The Center for Tomorrow's Company predicts that by 2025 the word "employee" will seem as dated as the term "domestic servant." Many companies have dispensed with "employees" and replaced them with "colleagues" and "associates."

Daily Telegraph, *14 January 2000*

INTERLUDE – THE WAY WE WORK

Here's a selection of items that have appeared in national newspapers over the last few years. They speak volumes about what people are thinking and feeling about the world of work.

"Company drivers clock up an annual total of estimated 8.2 billion unnecessary business miles with the sole purpose of minimizing their tax liability."

The Guardian, 17 January 1998

"Half the population meet their future partner at work."
Survey by the Industrial Society, April 1998

"A survey by *Accountancy Age* reveals that out of 600 accountants surveyed, 38% said they wish they had never gone into the profession."
The Mirror, 14 July 1999

"Over the past 10 years, the proportion of women returning to work after giving birth has risen from one-quarter to two-thirds."
The Independent, 7 October 1999

"Physical appearance counts in the workplace, according to a US survey. People rated as attractive are two to five times more likely to be taken on. They are also less likely to be laid off."
The Guardian, 25 March 2000

"A survey by HSBC Bank reports that one in four workers would give up 20% of their pay for an extra day off each week."
Daily Telegraph, 7 April 2000

"A survey by the Institute of Personnel and Development reveals that 40% of UK workers under 30 think it normal to change jobs every two or three years."
The Times, 13 April 2000

"A report by Office Angels has found that 70% of staff believe that the people they meet outside work judge them instantly by their job titles."
The Guardian, 18 April 2000

"Indian restaurants in the UK now employ more people than the steel, coal mining, and shipbuilding industries combined."
The Times, 18 May 2000

"According to a new survey, 91% of 1516 business managers questioned said that they worked longer than their contracted hours."
Financial Times, 2 February 2001

"Bosses at an Austrian car factory discovered that production was up 8% after painting the toilets bright pink and green. Workers hate the new color schemes so much that they now spend less time away from the production line."
News of the World, 22 March 2001

THE WAR FOR TALENT

Paradoxically, at the same time as companies unload people in droves, a yearlong study conducted by a team from McKinsey & Co., involving 77 companies and almost 6000 managers and executives, has suggested that the most important corporate resource over the next 20 years will be talent: smart, sophisticated business people who are technologically literate, globally astute, and operationally agile. And even as the demand for talent goes up, the supply of it will be going down.

The McKinsey team is blunt about what will result from these trends in its report, titled *The War for Talent*. The search for the best and the brightest will become a constant, costly battle. Not only will companies have to devise more imaginative recruitment practices; they will also have to work harder to keep their best people. In the new economy, competition is global, capital is abundant, ideas are developed quickly and cheaply, and people are willing to change jobs often. In that kind of environment, says Ed Michaels, a McKinsey director who helped manage the study, "all that matters is talent. Talent wins."

ZEITBITE

A survey in 1999 from the Institute of Directors and Development Dimensions International asked HR directors what percentage of their employees they would re-hire if they could change all their employees overnight. Half said they would re-hire between 0% and 40%.

THE END OF CAREERS 1

The career, as an institution, is in unavoidable decline according to a fascinating pamphlet[14] from independent UK think tank Demos. The authors describe two work patterns – the Wired and the Entrepreneurial – which might supplant the traditional career. In a nutshell, the Wired pattern replaces the lifelong identity of the career with a series of "brief habits," at the heart of which is spontaneity rather than continuity of projects and relationships. With the Entrepreneurial pattern, Flores and Gray widen out the narrow economic definition of entrepreneurship to include all manner of activities which initiate meaningful change in a context of shared responsibility. This could be in commerce, service or in society in general. The authors go on to examine these new forms of working life in some detail and consider the implications for individuals and communities. They conclude that core institutions – from education to pensions – need restructuring to support these changes.

THE END OF CAREERS 2

Tom Peters, co-author with Bob Waterman of *In Search of Excellence* in 1982, passionate believes that the individual has become the fundamental unit in the new economy. In recent years, he has focused increasingly on how changes at a corporate, national, and global level impact on the nature of work for us as individuals, and in August 1997, he contributed an article to *Fast Company* magazine called "The brand called you: you can't move up if you don't stand out." It's a brilliant synthesis of economic, marketing and business themes that ends with a stark conclusion:

> "It's this simple: you are a brand. You are in charge of your brand. There is no single path to success. And there is no one right way to create the brand called You. Except this: start today. Or else."

ZEITBITE

"In the future – the not-too-distant future – only two groups of people will be in the world of work: entrepreneurs and those who think like entrepreneurs."
Terri Lonier, CEO of Working Solo Inc., quoted in the Fast Take *newsletter, March 7, 2000*

NOTES

1 Pascale, R. (1990) *Managing on the Edge*, Simon & Schuster, New York.
2 Zuboff, S. (1998) *In the Age of the Smart Machine*, Basic Books, New York.

3 Klein, N. (2000) *No Logo*, Flamingo, London.

4 Handy, C. (1999) in *CBI News*, October. (From text of speech given by Handy at the CBI National Conference '99.)

5 Nicholson, N. (1998) "How hardwired is human behavior?" *Harvard Business Review*, July–August.

6 Nicholson, N. (2000) *Managing the Human Animal*, Texere, London.

7 Simmons, A. (1998) *Territorial Games*, Amacom, New York.

8 Survey by Management Today magazine and specialist consultancy WFD, quoted in *Daily Telegraph*, 24 September 1998.

9 Donnellon, A. (1996) *Team Talk*, Harvard Business School Press, Boston, MA.

10 This section was derived from ideas set out in Wallace, P. (1999) *Agequake*, Nicholas Brealey, New York.

11 Peters, T. (2000) "What will we do for work?" *Time* 29 May.

12 This section was derived from "The women and work survey," *The Economist*, 18 July 1998.

13 Hochschild, A.R. (1998) *The Time Bind: When Work becomes Home and Home becomes Work*, Metropolitan Books, New York.

14 Flores, F. & Gray, J. (2000) *Entrepreneurship and the Wired Life: Work in the Wake of Careers*, Demos, London.

Organizational Behavior in Practice

» Organizational behavior is about real people taking real actions that affect the well-being of their companies.
» Case studies: Dell Computer Corporation; Encyclopaedia Britannica; Sears; Sundaram-Clayton Limited; and The Natural Step.
» Common themes that emerge from these case studies.

"This ability to perceive the limitations of one's own culture and to develop the culture adaptively is the essence and ultimate challenge of leadership."[1]

Edgar Schein

"Today, the organization chart is hyperlinked, not hierarchical. Respect for hands-on knowledge wins over respect for abstract authority."[2]

Rick Levine, Christopher Locke, Doc Searls, and David Weinberger

There are a number of factors that can affect an organization's performance. These include:

» the formal statements of philosophy, values, charter, and credo;
» the behavior modeled by management;
» the criteria used for reward, status, selection, promotion, and termination;
» the stories, legends, myths, and parables about key people and events;
» what leaders pay attention to, measure, and control;
» leaders' reactions to critical incidents and crises that threaten survival, challenge norms, and test values;
» how the organization is designed and structured;
» organizational systems and procedures; and
» the competitive marketplace.

It is how organizations manage these elements during periods of transition that often seems to determine whether they achieve their goals. In this section, we will look at a number of organizations and how they have tackled – with varying levels of success – challenges facing their businesses. Each case study will be followed by a brief description of key lessons or insights to be drawn.

DELL COMPUTER CORPORATION

"It's easy to fall in love with how far you've come and how much you've done. It's definitely harder to see the cracks in a structure you've built yourself, but that's all the more reason to look hard and look often. Even if something seems to be working, it can be improved."[3]

Michael Dell, CEO, Dell Computer Corporation

The organization

By the age of 12, Michael Dell's entrepreneurial streak was beginning to emerge. That year, he earned $2000 from selling stamps. By the time he was 18, he was selling customized personal computers. He started the Dell Computer Corporation in 1984 with $1000, dropping out of his biology course at Austin University in Texas. The company, under his leadership, has gone on to become one of the most successful computer businesses in the world, redefining the industry with its direct-sale approach and the customer support model it pioneered. Dell himself is a member of the Board of Directors of the United States Chamber of Commerce and the ComputerWorld/Smithsonian Awards.

The story

Dell Computer Corporation is one of the computer industry's biggest success stories. Established in 1984, Michael Dell founded his company with the unprecedented idea of bypassing the middleman and selling custom-built computers direct to end users. His premise from the beginning was to under-promise and over-deliver – and that applied to customers, suppliers, and employees alike.

Originally an "offline" business, Dell was quick to appreciate the potential of the Internet – in fact, he built an e-business before anyone had even coined the term. Dell.com was a natural extension of the offline business. The site is customer- rather than product-focused, being aligned by customer categories, not hardware model lines. The site directs each different type of customer to the appropriate second-level page, where the relevant line of Dell products is presented.

Pursuing this customer orientation still further, Dell brings customers into the product planning and manufacturing processes, not just the sales process, and the management encourage everyone in the company to have contact with customers.

Here's how Michael Dell himself characterizes his business approach in his book *Direct from Dell.*[4]

» Think about the customer, not the competition. Competitors represent your industry's past, as, over the years, collective habits become ingrained. Customers are your future, representing new opportunities, ideas, and avenues for growth.

» Work to maintain a healthy sense of urgency and crisis. This doesn't mean that you want to fabricate deadlines or keep people so stressed that they quickly burn out. Set the bar slightly higher than you normally would, so that your people can achieve aggressive goals by working smarter.

» Be opportunistic, but also be fast. Look to find opportunity, especially when it isn't readily apparent. Focusing on the customer doesn't mean that you should ignore the competition. If something that your competition did or didn't do provided you with an opportunity today, would you recognize it and be able to act on it immediately? Today a competitive win can be decided literally one day at a time. You have to act fast, be ready, then be ready to change – fast.

» Be the hunter, not the hunted. Success is a dangerous thing, as we are at once invincible and vulnerable. Always strive to keep your team focused on growing the business and on winning and acquiring new business. Even though your company may be leading the market, you never want your people to act as though you are. That leads to complacency, and complacency kills. Encourage people to think "This is good. This worked. Now how can we take what we've proven and use it to win new business?" There's a big difference between asking that and asking "How can we defend our existing accounts?"

Analysis

Obsessive customer focus linked to strategic savvy and an ongoing commitment to innovation are clearly instrumental to Dell's success over the years, but just as important has been Michael Dell's commitment to internal organizational processes.

He has described culture as "one of the most enigmatic facets of management"[5] that he has encountered "and also one of the most important."

When asked which of his competitors represented the biggest threat to Dell, he said that the greatest threat wouldn't come from a competitor, it would come from the people who worked for Dell. His goal at Dell has been to make sure that everybody within the company feels they are a part of "something great – something special – perhaps something even greater than themselves." To achieve this, he set out from the beginning to create a company of owners. As he puts it in *Direct from Dell*:[6]

> "Creating a culture in which every person in your organization, at every level, thinks and acts like an owner means that you need to aim to connect individual performance with your company's most important objectives. For us, that means we mobilize everyone around creating the best possible customer experience and enhancing shareholder value – and we use specific quantifiable measurements of our progress towards those goals that apply to every employee's performance. A company composed of individual owners is less focused on hierarchy and who has the nicest office, and more intent on achieving their goals."

Simply put, Dell's approach is about establishing and maintaining a healthy, competitive culture by partnering with his people through shared objectives and a common strategy.

This is not just a lofty statement; it is backed up by a set of highly practical actions. When recruiting, for example, the company looks for people who are completely in synch with its business philosophy and objectives. Dell says: "If the person thinks in a way that's compatible with your company values and beliefs, and understands what the company does and is driven to do, he will not only work hard to fulfill his immediate goals, but he will also contribute to the greater goals of the organization." That's not to say that Dell encourages "herd" thinking – but that everyone in the company is mobilized around a customer-oriented focus.

Because of the constant demand for talent, recruiting is a non-stop, year-round activity, like R&D or sales. The result is a steady pipeline of talent. Dell doesn't recruit strictly for job openings; it hires the best available candidates, even if that means creating a new position. To quote Andy Esparza, the company's head of staffing, "Why would you choose not to hire a great person just because there's no job opening at the present time?"[7]

Dell Computers then has an intensely people-centric culture. For any company that wishes to emulate the Dell model, there seem to be six keys to their approach. These can be summed up as follows.

1 Mobilize your people around a common goal.
2 Invest in long-term goals by hiring ahead of the game and communicating this commitment to your people.
3 Don't leave the talent search to the human resources section – get personally involved as much as you can.
4 Cultivate a commitment to personal growth.
5 Build an infrastructure that rewards mastery – the best way to keep talented people is to allow their jobs to change with them.
6 Keep in touch with people at all levels of the company – immerse yourself in real information with real people.

ENCYCLOPAEDIA BRITANNICA INC.

The organization

The *Encyclopædia Britannica* was founded in 1768 in Edinburgh, Scotland, by Colin Macfarquhar, a printer, and Andrew Bell, an engraver. Now headquartered in Chicago, Illinois, Encyclopædia Britannica Inc. and Britannica.com Inc. describe themselves as leading providers of learning and knowledge products.

The story

Between 1990 and 1997, hardback sales of the *Encyclopaedia Britannica* more than halved. During the same period, sales of CD-ROMs blossomed. When Microsoft launched *Encarta*, it must have seemed like a toy to Britannica's executives, who knew that their encyclopedia's intellectual material was far superior to *Encarta*, whose content was derived from an encyclopedia traditionally sold at low cost in supermarkets. However, what the Britannica team failed to understand was that parents had bought their encyclopedia because they wanted to "do the right thing" for their children. In the 1990s, parents "do the right thing" by buying a computer. As far as the customer is concerned, *Encarta* is a near perfect substitute for *Britannica*.

Add to the equation the enormous cost advantage enjoyed by *Encarta* which can be produced for around £1 a copy, compared with around £200 to produce a set of *Britannica*, and the recipe for *Britannica*'s downfall was complete.

Analysis

The arrival of new, Internet-based firms that are more agile and innovative than the giants is upsetting many a corporate applecart. The Internet is helping to put small, agile newcomers on a par with large corporations and able to compete head-on with them for new business. Just as Microsoft could appear from virtually nowhere to usurp the market of mighty IBM, so a few years later Netscape appeared overnight and threatened to undermine the market (and the size) of Microsoft. Who will be next? And where will they come from? In this world, small agile firms have an advantage over giant organizations that are unable to take decisions quickly. This process will accelerate as more and more companies join the e-commerce bandwagon.

The story of Britannica is a demonstration of how quickly the new economics of information have changed the rules of competition. Some might therefore argue that Britannica's woes could be ascribed simply to a set of poor strategic choices.

From a cultural perspective, the deeper question is not simply what mistakes the company made, but rather why those mistakes occurred. The Britannica story is a parable about the dangers of complacency. The fact that a company has been around for over 200 years doesn't grant it any special rights over its competitors; and yet the company's leaders did seem to assume that they were impervious to external developments.

It has taken Britannica four years to begin to recover its position. These days, the company has set its sights on making full use of all new media, including wireless, to make rich information available to people wherever they need it. The company is also actively syndicating some of its more popular features throughout the Internet, making *Britannica* information more widely accessible. In 2001, BritannicaSchool.com made its debut as a broad educational service that combines high-quality reference materials with electronic curriculum programs designed to make learning engaging and enjoyable.

GALLUP'S PICTURE OF ORGANIZATIONAL HEALTH

A recent issue of *Fast Company*[8] magazine reported how The Gallup Organization undertook an exercise to process 30 years' worth of data on worker attitudes to try and answer one simple but crucial question: "What does a strong and vibrant workplace look like?"

From their analysis, project leader Marcus Buckingham and his team distilled 12 core issues (called the "Q12") that act as an effective barometer of the strength of any work unit.

The Q12 questions

According to Marcus Buckingham, these are the 12 factors that determine whether people are engaged, not engaged, or actively disengaged at work.

1 Do I know what is expected of me at work?
2 Do I have the materials and equipment that I need in order to do my work right?
3 At work, do I have the opportunity to do what I do best every day?
4 In the past seven days, have I received recognition or praise for doing good work?
5 Does my supervisor, or someone at work, seem to care about me as a person?
6 Is there someone at work who encourages my development?
7 At work, do my opinions seem to count?
8 Does the mission or purpose of my company make me feel that my job is important?
9 Are my co-workers committed to doing quality work?
10 Do I have a best friend at work?
11 In the past six months, has someone at work talked to me about my progress?
12 This past year, have I had opportunities at work to learn and grow?

Next, the team set about analyzing how the answers given to the Q12 linked to concrete business effectiveness measures. They found that the most "engaged" workplaces were 50% more likely to have lower turnover, 56% more likely to have higher-than-average customer loyalty, 38% more likely to have above-average productivity, and 27% more likely to report higher profitability.

Buckingham's team made another startling discovery: there was more variation in scores *within* companies than *between* companies. In other words, Buckingham found some of the most-engaged groups and some of the least-engaged groups working within the same company. On top of that, CEOs typically were not aware who in their company was engaged effectively and who wasn't.

SEARS

The organization

The company's history dates back to the 1880s, when Richard Sears was an agent of the Minneapolis and St Louis railway station in North Redwood, Minnesota. Sears' job as station agent left him plenty of spare time, so he sold lumber and coal to local residents on the side to make extra money. Sears set up a mail order business in the 1890s. The company opened its first retail store in 1925; numbers rapidly grew and by 1997 there were over 800 stores.

Today, the company's mission statement is: *Sears: a compelling place to shop, to work, and to invest.*

The story

In 1992, Sears announced it would again reshape the company to give it greater strength and marketing focus and to give its shareholders a better return on investment.

As part of this restructuring, the Sears Merchandise Group, reorganized around its apparel, home, and automotive business, closed many of its under-performing department stores as well as its specialty stores. Its unprofitable catalog merchandise distribution operations were also closed in 1993, leaving a smaller – but successful – direct-response business.

Led by CEO Arthur Martinez, a group of more than 100 top-level Sears executives spent three years rebuilding the company around its customers. In rethinking what Sears was and what it wanted to become, these managers developed a business model of the company and an accompanying measurement system that tracks success from management behavior through employee attitudes to customer satisfaction and financial performance.

Analysis

Over the past five years, Sears has radically changed the way it does business and dramatically improved its financial results. But Sears' transformation was more than a change in marketing strategy. It was also a change in the logic and culture of the business. The company has been rebuilt around its customers using a business model and accompanying performance measures that track success through employee attitudes to customer satisfaction and financial performance. One problem for Sears was measuring such soft data as "customer satisfaction." However, by means of an ongoing process of data collection, analysis, modelling, and experimentation Sears not only achieved this but also changed the way in which mangers think and behave. This cultural change is now spreading throughout the company.[9]

SUNDARAM-CLAYTON LIMITED

"Our human resources and learning from the best practices across the world has made us an organization poised for a quantum leap."
C. Narasimhan, President, Sundaram-Clayton Limited

The organization

Established in 1962 in collaboration with Clayton Dewandre Holdings plc, Sundaram-Clayton Ltd (SCL) is an Indian company that has pioneered the manufacture of air-assisted and air brake systems for home-based commercial vehicles. With a commitment of total satisfaction to customers, the company has achieved a share of business in the Original Equipment segment of over 85% and a market share in the sales aftermarket of around 75%.

The story

This is the story of a company operating in a country without a strong track record in manufacture that has pursued Total Quality Management (TQM) principles to become globally recognized. The company's commitment to TQM is very apparent from its mission statement:

> "We at SCL are all set to lead the automotive air braking business in Asia with a foundation built on continuous innovation and commitment to uncompromising quality. Our dedication towards customer satisfaction has enabled us to stay ahead of competition. Our principles of quality, service, and reliability have instilled in us the strength to drive on the export market with confidence. At SCL, we take our responsibilities as a corporate citizen seriously by contributing actively to the development of the local communities. Total Quality Management is a way of life with us. SCL respects the individual and believes in encouraging its employees by creating the ambience they need to achieve self-actualization.
>
> We are committed to being a profitable and socially responsible leading manufacturer of environmentally friendly auto components and sub-systems for customers in global markets and to provide fulfillment and prosperity for customers, employees and vendors."

SCL's commitment to enhancing customer satisfaction through continuous improvement and total employee involvement led the company to a significant milestone – The Deming Award. In 1998, SCL's Brakes division was awarded the prestigious prize for achieving "distinctive performance improvement through the application of company-wide quality control." As most people know, the examination procedures and selection process for the award are exacting and elaborate, and so it was a real achievement for SCL, particularly as it was only the fourth organization in the world outside Japan to win this prize, and the first in India.

Analysis

For years, India's reputation for manufacturing has been undermined by Nehru's declaration that "It is better to have a second-rate thing made in one's own country than a first-rate thing one has to import."

SCL believes differently. Although its quality systems have attracted most public attention, SCL has a people-centric outlook. An approach SCL calls Total Employee Involvement (TEI) forms the base of the company's quest for excellence through TQM. According to C. Narasimhan, president of SCL:

> "At SCL we are poised to achieve breakthroughs by realizing the importance of continuously honing the expertise of our human resources and learning from the best practices across the world. Tremendous importance is accorded on the training and retraining of not only our employees but also our vendors and end-users."

It is this borrowing and incorporating of best practices from around the world that has enabled the company to escape a national attitude personified by Nehru's famous comment, and this, says Narasimhan, "has made us an organization poised for a quantum leap."

The company has also heavily influenced the work practices of its Indian suppliers. A report in the *Economist*[10] tells how Jagadeesan Industries, a 32-employee strong company whose only customer is SCL, has itself incorporated total quality management principles in its tiny factory in Chennai. Machine operators have "ownership" of the components they make, which means that they, not a supervisor, are in charge of quality control.

Under pressure from SCL to upgrade their quality and speed up deliveries without raising prices, the management at Jagadeesan realized that this could only be achieved by abandoning a traditional set of management practices that F.W. Taylor would have recognized and doubtless approved of.

This is how the *Economist* describes Jagadeesan's transformation:

> "Before, everything was secret" from the workers, says J. Selvam, one of Jagadeesan's owners. Now the workers have a lot more information: not only on matters relating to their own jobs, but also

on the firm's turnover and profits. They are paid unprincely salaries of 900–2750 rupees, but they are now supplied with uniforms and meals and such formal-sector benefits as contributions made for them to the public-sector pension scheme, says Mr Selvam.

THE NATURAL STEP

The organization

The Natural Step (TNS) is a non-profit environmental education organization working to build an ecologically and economically sustainable society. The Natural Step offers a framework that is based on science and serves as a compass for businesses, communities, academia, government entities, and individuals working to redesign their activities to become more sustainable. Today, TNS has offices in Australia, Canada, Japan, New Zealand, South Africa, Sweden, the United Kingdom, and the United States.

The stated purpose of TNS is "To develop and share a common framework comprised of easily understood, scientifically based principles that can serve as a compass to guide society towards a just and sustainable future."

The story

In Sweden, a group of professional associations, involving some 10,000 people, has formed a large-scale social and environmental movement called The Natural Step. The associations and their members co-operate on projects that work towards developing a sustainable society. Karl-Henrik Robèrt describes how sustainability provides a shared sense of purpose that binds the associate members together, allowing them to create large-scale change.

"What binds [us] together is a collective understanding of the larger system of which we are a part. A system is like a tree – the trunk and the branches are the underlying principles that give form and structure to the system, while the leaves represent the various efforts we can take to meet the principles.

"The various associations – the engineers and scientists, doctors, and lawyers – are each operating as the leaves, providing input from their background, while the trunk provides an overarching unity to our work."[11]

The Natural Step Framework helps individuals and organizations address key environmental issues from a systems perspective, reduce the use of natural resources, develop new technologies, and facilitate better communications among employees and members. It gives people a common language and guiding principles to help change existing practices and decrease their impact on the environment. The system conditions have been used as a shared mental model for problem-solving; for the development of consensus documents (e.g. sustainable practices with regard to metals, energy, agriculture, and forestry); to structure institutional scientific work at universities and in course curricula for the teaching of students; and by business corporations, municipalities, and other organizations as an instrument for strategic planning towards sustainability.

Analysis

It is the ability of an organization to create a shared sense of purpose and vision that enables large numbers of people to work together in a co-ordinated way. True vision occurs only when an organization really understands where it wants to go and these aspirations become its *primary organizing principle*.

TNS encourages dialog and consensus-building, a key process of learning organizations. The Natural Step Framework is based on systems thinking, focusing on first-order principles at the beginning of cause–effect relationships.

CORE SKILLS IN PRACTICE: THINKING BETTER BY LISTENING MORE ATTENTIVELY

Over the past 17 years, Nancy Kline has developed a system called a Thinking Environment™, a model of human interaction that dramatically improves the way people think – and thus work and live. Listening – defined by Kline as the quality of people's attention for each other – is the core of this method. Here, in a brief extract from her book *Time to Think*,[12] is an example of how people, when managed effectively, can talk themselves into lucidity:

"Organizations intimidate people into believing that 'the higher up you are in a hierarchy, the better you can think.' And welding this assumption to the floor of the mind of managers is the assumption that to seek out ideas from people junior to you is to look incompetent. The absurdity of this is obvious – often the people near the top, because of their isolation from what is really happening, have less chance of thinking well than most of the people junior to them – but the assumption persists nevertheless.

"Not, however, at Staples, the office supplies company. One of the divisional managers has done a good thing. She has institutionalized equality of thinking in the workplace. She has set up a forum for ideas, a bi-monthly meeting with all levels of her staff. She gathers them in groups of about 12 (which, by the way, is about as big as you can make a group and still expect it to be safe enough for people to say what they think. Organizations that gather 200 employees to announce policy changes and then open the floor to questions and comments from the audience are, in effect, not holding an open consultative forum at all. Most people will not stand up to speak in a group of colleagues that large).

"The Staples manager poses two questions:

"1 What have you noticed that needs attention or change in this company that I might not have noticed?

"2 What do you think should be done about it?

"Then she sits down and listens. Everyone speaks without rush or interruption. She makes notes, asks clarifying questions only, does not challenge their ideas or defend herself. She promises to think about each one. She does not promise to do everything people suggest, but she does agree to let them know what she decides to do with their ideas and why. This takes time, but she claims it has gained time overall because embers have been snuffed before they combusted, new paths she had never thought of have opened up, and employee involvement and commitment have increased – those two unmeasurable soft qualities on which so much of the hard stuff depends.

"Equality is particularly a feature in any Thinking Environment meeting. Many times during the meeting, including at the beginning and at the end, everyone has a turn to speak. Every person is considered equally valuable. The chair or other people in authority may have to make the final decisions; not every meeting can work effectively on consensus. But the chance to contribute ideas and points of view is given equally in a Thinking Environment."

BEST PRACTICE: PULLING IT ALL TOGETHER

So what can we conclude from the case studies in this section? Here are five key themes that run through the examples we have looked at.

Companies mirror their founders

Edgar Schein has described how organizations start with founders and entrepreneurs whose personal assumptions and values gradually create a certain way of thinking and operating, and if their companies are successful, those ways of thinking and operating come to be taken for granted as the "right" way to run a business. Michael Dell's personal stamp is all over his company.

It is crisis, not comfort, that propels significant cultural change

When all is going well for a business, changing the formula is often the last thing on anybody's mind. The management at Jagadeesan seemed perfectly happy with their former set of working practices until they came under pressure from SCL to make a step improvement in the quality of service provided for no extra cost. Likewise, Encyclopaedia Britannica needed to be shaken up by a competitor before it could accept the reality that longevity is no guarantor of survival.

Achieving business success requires a sense of purpose first and good management practices second

An organization is not a club – its purpose is not solely to look after the well-being of its members.

Different strokes for different folks

Organizations achieve success in very different ways and by focusing on what is most important to them. For Dell, the focus was on culture. SCL achieved success by pursuing quality standards and adopting Western management practices.

In some cases, the need is to focus on dangers within the organization. For Encyclopaedia Britannica, the enemy was mindset.

There is no such thing as the ideal set of organizational behaviors or management practices, except in relation to what the organization is trying to do. A team of fire fighters will necessarily have a different set of operating patterns to an advertising agency. Even though our personality and preferences might make us better suited to work in some places rather than others, this doesn't make one environment automatically "better" than another.

On a similar tack, different people look for different things out of their careers. Some people look mainly for a sense of security and stability, while others seek out roles with a high level of challenge. Some want to manage people and resources; others prefer to pursue roles requiring a high level of technical competence.

Let's do this thing

Successful companies are those that came up with a way forward that is timely, credible, simple, and – most crucial of all – able to be readily applied. In the final analysis, organizational success comes down to implementation. The best ideas poorly executed are worthless.

NOTES

1 Schein, E. (1992) *Organizational Culture and Leadership*, 2nd edn, Jossey-Bass, San Francisco.
2 Levine, R. Locke, C., Searls, D. & Weinberger, D. (2000) *The Cluetrain Manifesto: The End of Business as Usual*, Perseus Publishing, New York.

3 Dell, M. (1999) *Direct from Dell*, HarperCollinsBusiness, New York.

4 *Ibid.*

5 *Ibid.*

6 *Ibid.*

7 Taken from Salter, C. (1999) "Talent – Andy Esparza," *Fast Company*, December, p.216.

8 Taken from LaBarre, P. (2001) "Marcus Buckingham thinks your boss has an attitude problem,"*Fast Company*, August, p.88.

9 For more background, please refer to: Rucci, A.J., Kirn, S.P. & Quinn, R.T (1998) "The employee-customer profit chain at Sears," *Harvard Business Review*, January–February.

10 See (2001) "The unknown majority," *Economist*, 2 June. (www.economist.com/displayStory.cfm?Story_ID=S%26%288%20% 2BRQ%23%20%0A)

11 Robèrt, K.-H. (1995) "The natural step: a framework for large-scale change," *The Systems Thinker*, October.

12 Kline, N. (1999) *Time to Think*, Ward Lock, London.

Key Concepts and Thinkers

- » Glossary of organizational behavior.
- » Key thinkers.

"Organizational behavior is in reality a hodgepodge of various subjects; a collection of loosely related or even unrelated streams of scholarly and not-so-scholarly research."[1]

Jack Wood

GLOSSARY OF ORGANIZATIONAL BEHAVIOR

Like many other business subjects, the theory and practice of organizational behavior have a language all their own. Here is a selective glossary of some of the key terms, key concepts and key thinkers associated with the subject.

Action learning – Term coined by Reg Revans to describe an approach in which learning is installed by dealing with real life business problems, rather than through formal courses.

Adhocracy – A non-bureaucratic networked organization with a highly organic organizational design.

Artifacts – Artifacts are everything we might see, hear, or feel within an organization. They include: the physical environment; all visible behaviors; the way people dress; rituals and ceremonies; published documents; the technology used; commonly used language and jargon; status symbols such as cars; job titles; and so on.

Bureaucracy – A term coined by Max Weber. In a bureaucracy, laws, rules, procedures, and predefined routines are dominant, and the exercise of "due process" all important. The term has come to be associated with organizations which have over-complicated procedures and trivial rules.

Business process redesign – This involves changing both organizational structure and processes to ensure that future customer needs can be anticipated and fulfilled in the most cost-effective manner. It should not be confused with crude cost-cutting exercises (such as downsizing), although many organizations have used both approaches simultaneously, with the result that the value of process redesign has been tarnished in the eyes of many managers.

Codification strategy and personalization strategy – Part of the burgeoning language of knowledge management. In companies that sell relatively standardized products that fill common needs, knowledge is carefully codified and stored in databases, where it can be accessed and used again and again by anyone in the organization.

This is a *codification strategy*. In companies that provide highly customized solutions to unique problems, knowledge is shared mainly through person-to-person contacts; the chief purpose of computers is to help people communicate. This is a *personalization strategy*.

Communities of practice – Groups that form within an organization, typically of their own accord, where members are drawn to one other by a common set of needs that may be both professional and social. Compared to project teams, communities of practice are voluntary, longer-lived, have no specific deliverable, and are responsible only to themselves. Because they are free of formal strictures and hierarchy within an organization, they can be viewed as subversive.

Contingency theory – According to this theory, there is no one best way to organize how a business operates. Each organization has to address its own unique set of circumstances.

Core competencies – The key strengths of an organization (sometimes called distinctive capabilities). Gary Hamel and C.K. Prahalad, authors of *Competing for the Future*, define core competencies as "a bundle of skills and technologies (rather than a simple or discrete skill or technology) that enables the company to provide a particular benefit to customers."

Core competents – The small number of people in an organization who are absolutely vital to that organization's success. Bill Gates has reflected that if 20 people were to leave Microsoft, the company would risk bankruptcy. In a study by the Corporate Leadership Council, a computer firm recognized 100 "core competents" out of 16,000 employees; a software company had 10 out of 11,000; and a transportation group deemed 20 of its 33,000 as really critical.

Covert culture – Term coined by Gerard Egan, professor of organization development and psychology at Loyola University of Chicago, to describe those elements of organizational culture that are, in his words "not in the private consciousness of the members of the institution, not in the public consciousness of members of the institution, not written down, not named or noted in some public forum, only partially understood, not celebrated in some public way, not discussed in any public forum, not challenged or perhaps not even open to challenge, considered undiscussible in public forums and at times so undiscussible that even their undiscussibility is undiscussible."

Cultural fit – Building and sustaining a corporate culture that fits your needs requires a critical mass of employees who are committed to the culture's core beliefs and values. It is much easier to hire people with those traits than to change their personalities, beliefs, and behaviors once they are hired. Ask questions in the interviews and listen carefully to their stories about previous work experiences. Listen for cultural fit: you may be hiring the technical or professional skills you need but damaging your chances of building a strong culture.

Cultural integration – Some companies have a strong dominant culture that is pervasive throughout the organization across business units and regions. An organization of this type is said to possess a high level of cultural integration.

Cultural web – A useful concept in which the organization is understood in terms of the routines, rituals, stories, structures, and systems that exist within it. It can be used to elicit the organizational paradigm because each component of the cultural web provides clues about taken-for-granted organizational assumptions.

Culture carriers – People in an organization that is going through a period of change who see the new direction and feel comfortable moving in that direction.

Desk rage – Long hours and the growing pressures of the workplace are leading to increasing outbreaks of office strife or "desk rage." As stress builds in the office, workers are increasingly venting their frustrations on colleagues.

Discontinuities – One-off changes in the marketplace that force radical organizational change.

Distinctive capabilities – See *Core competencies*

Downshifting – The deliberate decision by somebody to simplify their life by, for example, balancing work and home life, or reducing levels of financial commitment, at the expense of income.

Downsizing – Restructuring an organization in a declining market where the level of resources (manpower, support functions, etc.) are inappropriate to meeting current customer needs.

E-lancers – Independent contractors connected through personal computers and electronic networks. These electronically connected freelancers join together into fluid and temporary networks to produce and sell goods and services.

Emotional intelligence – A concept popularized by Daniel Goleman that refers to our capacity for recognizing our own feelings and those of others, for motivating ourselves, and for managing emotions in ourselves and in our relationships.

Espoused values – This is what an organization says it believes. Sometimes this will be manifest in the artifacts of the organization, for example, an espoused value that open communication is important may show itself in the form of regular briefings for employees, or the way an office is laid out, or in the content of the corporate mission statement. Sometimes, however, these values will be espoused but not enacted. These moments of discrepancy between what an organizations says it believes and what it does in practice are in themselves highly indicative of the type of organizational culture that prevails.

Force field analysis – A technique which enables the factors supporting and working against change to be identified and assessed in terms of their significance.

Globalization – The integration of economic activity across national or regional boundaries, a process that has been accelerated by the impact of information technology.

Hawthorne studies – Conducted in the 1920s, these landmark studies showed how work groups didn't respond to classical motivational approaches, as suggested in the scientific management approach, but rather that workers were also interested in the rewards and punishments of their own work group.

Hierarchy – A system for classifying organizational roles and the people who fill them in terms of their rank or importance.

Human Relations Movement – In part a reaction to the scientific management school, advocates of this approach emphasize people rather than machines. Human relations draws its inspiration from biological rather than engineering systems.

Informate – Term coined by Harvard academic Shoshana Zuboff to describe the capacity for information technology to translate and make visible organizational processes, objects, behaviors, and events.

Intellectual capital – Intellectual material knowledge, information, intellectual property, experience that can be put to use to create wealth. In a business context, the sum total of what employees in an organization know that gives it a competitive edge.

Internal capabilities or competencies – What the organization is good at. Something an organization can do that its potential competitors cannot.

Internal constraints – Factors that can inhibit an organization's ability to achieve desired outcomes. These factors include the level of resources available, knowledge of new markets and products, the cultural adaptability of the organization to new opportunities, etc.

Key Performance Indicators (KPIs) – Normally combined as a basket of measures to cover all critical areas of the organization. Although the choice of specific indicators will depend on the unique circumstances of the organization, KPIs are generally selected from the following categories of information: customer satisfaction; product and service innovation; operational improvement; employee morale and commitment; financial health; and cultural diagnosis.

Knowledge management – A system, most often computer-based, to share information in a company with the goal of increasing levels of responsiveness and innovation.

Learning organization – Peter Senge characterizes learning organizations as places where "people continually expand their capacity to create the results they truly desire, where new and expansive patterns of thinking are nurtured, where collective aspiration is set free, and where people are continually learning how to learn together." He also acknowledges that the idea of a learning organization is a vision.

Meme – First coined by Richard Dawkins when updating Darwin's theory of natural selection in his groundbreaking book *The Selfish Gene* (1976), a meme is an idea, behavior, or skill that can be transferred from one person to another by imitation. Memes are replicators and are all around us in our everyday lives, competing to get into our brains and minds. Examples include the way in which we copy ideas, inventions, songs, catch-phrases, and stories from one another.

Micro-careers – With the death of the job-for-life went the notion of getting paid to do broadly the same thing throughout your working days. Micro-careers are those distinct and separate chunks of activity that will characterize an individual's working life in the twenty-first century.

Motivation – The internal needs that drive or energize behavior.

Organizational behavior (OB) – The study of human behavior, attitudes and performance within an organizational setting. OB draws on theory, methods, and principles from such disciplines as psychology, sociology, and cultural anthropology to learn about individual perception, values, learning capabilities, and actions while working with groups and within the total organization. OB also can involve analyzing the external environment's effect on the organization and its learning resources, missions, objectives, and strategies.

Organizational culture – Defined by Edgar Schein, a professor at MIT who is considered one of the "founders" of organizational psychology, as "a pattern of shared basic assumptions that the group learned as it solved its problems of external adaptation and internal integration, that has worked well enough to be considered valid and, therefore, to be taught to new members as the correct way to perceive, think, and feel in relation to those problems. Schein's definition brings together many of the ideas and concepts expressed in that earlier list of definitions, but puts particular emphasis on shared, taken-for-granted, basic assumptions held by the member of the group or organization.

Organization development (OD) – According to Richard Beckhard, writing in his book *Organization Development: Strategies and Models*, "OD is an effort that is (1) planned, (2) organization-wide, and (3) managed from the top, to increase (4) organizational effectiveness and health, through (5) planned interventions in the organization's 'processes,' using behavioral-science knowledge."

Paradigm – A constellation of concepts, values, perceptions and practices shared by a community which form a particular vision of reality and collective mood that is the basis of the way that the community organizes itself.

PYMWYMIC – A company that acts according to its values and beliefs, as in a "Put Your Money Where Your Mouth Is Company."

Reality check – A reality check is any tool, technique, method, or device used by an individual or organization to provide feedback on their place in the world. Reality checks include tools and techniques that are recognized as "strategic" (such as industry analysis, competitor analysis, and so on) and many others that are not (customer research, employee feedback, or merely reading trade magazines).

Scientific management – An approach to work devised around a century ago by F.W. Taylor that involved detailed observation and measurement of even the most routine work to find the optimum mode of performance. Taylor advocated the use of time-and-motion study as a means of analyzing and standardizing work activities.

Seven S model – Widely used analytical tool, devised by Richard Pascale and Anthony Athos, that evaluates organizations under seven key headings to which managers need to pay attention. The seven are: strategy, structure, systems, skills, style, shared values, and staff. Some of these areas are "hard" (i.e. strategy, structure, and systems) and some are "soft" (style, staff, and shared values). "Skills" is placed center-stage because it is both "hard" and "soft," comprising both the distinctive capabilities of key personnel and the core competencies of the organization as a whole.

Shared vision – In a corporation, a shared vision changes people's relationship with the company. It is no longer "their company;" it becomes "our company." A shared vision is the first step in allowing people who mistrusted each other to begin to work together. It creates a common identity.

Subcultures – Very often, the culture in large organizations is not pervasive, singular, or uniform. In these organizations, there is not one single culture but a collection of subcultures. Subcultures may share certain characteristics, norms, values, and beliefs or be totally different. These subcultures can function co-operatively or be in conflict with each other.

Theory X and Theory Y – Based on research conducted by Douglas McGregor, this theory suggests that managers are likely to believe one of two sets of assumptions about human behavior. A Theory X manager believes that work is inherently distasteful to most people, that people are not creative or ambitious and that they need to be closely managed by a mix of control and coercion. In contrast, Theory Y managers take the view that people can be self-directed and creative at work if properly motivated.

Underlying assumptions – Basic assumptions that have become so taken for granted that people in the organization would find it inconceivable to base their behavior on anything else. For example, a company's deeply-held belief that the customer should always be treated with respect would render it almost impossible that organizational employees would set out to deliberately rip off customers. These deeply-held assumptions are rarely articulated and even more rarely are they questioned unless some form of organizational crisis forces their re-examination.

Virtual organization – An organizational form that consists of a loose (and often temporary) combination of technology, expertise, and networks.

Vision – A company's view of its future that is compelling and stretching, but that is also viewed as achievable. A corporate vision for the future has to be grounded in awareness. If not, it quickly becomes a wish-driven strategy meritorious in all respects except for the fact that it will never be achieved.

KEY THINKERS

The following have been particularly influential in the field of organizational behavior. Many of their contributions are mentioned elsewhere in this book.

Drucker, Peter

When Peter Drucker wrote *The Concept of the Corporation* in 1945, he could find only two firms that offered management training to their staff, and only three academic courses that covered the subject. Since then, of course, the management business has boomed, and Drucker has gone on to become, in the words of the *Economist*, "the greatest thinker management theory has produced." Opinion has long been divided about Drucker. Now in his nineties, he still commands more respect than affection in some quarters and even that respect is tempered by a sense that his work lacks academic credibility. Interestingly, it is largely in the community of practicing managers that Drucker's reputation has been built. Perhaps that is because he has always written from the standpoint that the world of work is essentially about human endeavor.

Fayol, Henri

Perhaps more than anybody, Henri Fayol (1841–1925), a mining engineer and manager by profession, defined the nature and working patterns of the twentieth-century organization. In his book, *General and Industrial Management*, published in 1916, Fayol laid down 14 principles of management (see Chapter 3). Fayol also characterized the activities of a commercial organization into six basic elements: technical, commercial, financial, security, accounting, and management. The management function, Fayol believed, consisted of planning, organizing, commanding, co-ordinating, and controlling. Many practicing managers today would probably identify similar elements as the core of their activities.

Handy, Charles

Writer, lecturer, broadcaster, and self-styled social philosopher. In his 1989 book *The Age of Unreason*, he anticipated the growth of outsourcing, telecommuting, the intellectual capital movement, and the rise of knowledge workers *inter alia*; he also foresaw how these developments might impact on the individual. It was his concept of the portfolio worker that arguably provided a way forward for the downshifting movement of the 1990s.

Herzberg, Frederick

In his book *Motivation to Work* (1959), Herzberg coined the terms *hygiene factors* and *motivational factors* as a basis for exploring what motivated people to work well and happily.

Hofstede, Geert

Born in the Netherlands in 1928, Hofstede is currently Emeritus professor of organizational anthropology and international management at Maastricht University. He is best known for his work on four dimensions of cultural variability, commonly referred to as *Hofstede's Dimensions*.

Jaques, Elliott

For over 50 years, Jaques has consistently advocated the need for a scientific approach to understanding work systems. He argues that there is a "widespread, almost universal, underestimation of the impact of organization on how we go about our business." He believes, for example, that rapid change in people's behavior is achieved less through altering their psychological make-up and more by revising organizational structures and managerial leading practices. His book *Requisite Organization* challenges many current assumptions about effective organizations, particularly in the field of hierarchy – of which Jaques is a fan. Some find his theories indigestible, but for those who persist there is a wealth of challenging material that undermines much conventional organizational wisdom.

Maslow, Abraham

One of the most widely-known experts on human behavior and motivation, his psychological perspectives on management, such as the hierarchy of needs, are still studied today in business schools all over the world. Maslow's most influential business book, *Eupsychian Management*, is a stimulating but not always easy read that demonstrates clearly why he was an unparalleled thinker and innovator in applying human behavior to the workplace.

Morgan, Gareth

A Professor at York University in Toronto, Morgan is a best-selling author, speaker, and consultant on managing change. He argues that the use of metaphor – for example, likening an organization to a machine – can be helpful in revealing aspects of organizational life. For the use of metaphor implies a way of thinking and a way of seeing that pervades how we understand our world generally. In his book *Images of Organization*, he explores a rich and range of metaphors (organizations as organisms, as brains, as cultures, as psychic prisons, as political systems, etc.).

Pascale, Richard

Born in 1938, Richard Pascale was a member of the faculty of Stanford's Graduate School of Business for 20 years. Now a leading business consultant, he has written or co-authored three highly challenging books – *The Art of Japanese Management* (1981), *Managing on the Edge* (1990), and *Surfing on the Edge of Chaos* (2000).

Peters, Tom

Former McKinsey consultant and co-author (with Bob Waterman) of *In Search of Excellence* (1982), the most popular management book of recent times with global sales of over six million copies.

Schein, Edgar

Born in 1928, and a Professor at the MIT Sloan School of Management, Edgar H. Schein is sometimes seen as the "inventor" of the idea of corporate culture. More recently, his work has explored the nature of the psychological contract between employer and employee, and also career anchors – the idea that we each have an underlying career value that we are unwilling to give up.

Taylor, Frederick W

The world's first efficiency expert and "the father of scientific management." Taylor's work with car-making legend Henry Ford led directly to the mass production techniques that created 15 million Model Ts between 1910 and 1927, and that set the pattern for industrial working practice worldwide.

Weber, Max

Weber (1864–1920) was a German university professor who was the first person to describe organizations as having the qualities of a machine, a metaphor that persisted throughout the twentieth century. Weber is sometimes described, unfairly, as the father of bureaucracy.

NOTE

1 Wood, J. (1997) "Deep roots and far from a soft option," In: Bickerstaffe, G. (ed.), *Mastering Management*, FT/Pitman Publishing, London, pp.217–224.

Resources

» Books.
» Articles.
» Journals, magazines, and Websites.

Countless words have been written about what goes on in and around organizations. This chapter identifies some of the best resources around, including books, articles, journals and magazines, and Websites.

BOOKS: AN ANNOTATED BIBLIOGRAPHY

Over the years, literally thousands of books have been published directly or indirectly about human behavior within organizations. Here is a list of some of the best:

» **Adams, S. (1996) *The Dilbert Principle*, HarperBusiness, New York.**

Not since the early days of *The Far Side* by Gary Larson has there been a cartoon strip to match Dilbert, a mouthless, bespectacled computer nerd whose observations on modern business life are poignant, irreverent, and painfully funny. For workers around the world, Dilbert has become an essential part of their lives, a touchstone with reality when the world around them seems to be going crazy, and a mouthpiece for their unvoiced concerns and feelings. If you are not familiar with the work of Scott Adams, sample one of the Dilbert anthologies (*Build a Better Life by Stealing Office Supplies* is a very good starting point) and you will soon be smitten.

» **Back, K. & Back, K. (1991) *Assertiveness at Work*, McGraw-Hill, Maidenhead, UK.**

The book sets out a number of ways in which people can handle difficult situations at work more effectively. For those who find handling awkward situations, well, awkward, this is one of the best introductions to assertiveness techniques around. Equally, there are plenty of practical tips and suggestions for the more self-confident.

» **Badaracco, J. (1997) *Defining Moments*, Harvard Business School Press, Boston, MA.**

Defining Moments is a book about work and life choices and the critical points at which the two become one. It examines the conflicts that every manager faces and presents an unorthodox yet practical way for managers to think about and resolve them. Drawing on philosophy and literature, and built around three stories of real-life quandaries of increasing complexity that managers have faced as their careers have advanced, the book provides tangible examples, actionable steps, and a flexible framework that managers at all levels can use to make the choices that will shape not only their careers but their characters.

» **Bohm D. (ed. Nichol, L.) (1998)** *On Creativity*, **Routledge, London.**

A collection of five previously unpublished or unavailable essays on the nature of creativity by the late and distinguished physicist David Bohm. Much of the material draws overtly from Bohm's perceptions as a practicing scientist. In case you are wondering why a book like this could possibly be of interest to the business community, it is worthwhile pointing out that Peter Senge, author of *The Fifth Discipline* (the first book to popularize the concept of the learning organization), has publicly credited Bohm with influencing his thinking about team learning. Those with a particular interest in the use of dialog as a mode of learning and enquiry will be fascinated by the chapter entitled *Art, dialogue, and the implicate order.*

» **Caracciolo, A. (1999)** *Smart Things to Know about Teams*, **Capstone, Oxford.**

Smart Things to Know about Teams is an intelligently assembled overview of the latest thinking about teams and team working. Annemarie Caracciolo clearly knows her topic and draws eclectically on a wide range of sources – from Senge to St Luke's and from Warren Bennis to The Bishopston Team, a team of seven women who work as community midwives. Those readers who are already steeped in the subject may find little in the book that is truly groundbreaking, but for anybody looking for a one-stop overview of the subject, *Smart Things to Know about Teams* probably can't be bettered.

» **Chandler, R. & Grzyb, J.E. (1997)** *The Nice Factor Book*, **Simon and Schuster, London.**

Ever apologized even when you haven't done anything wrong? Do you have friends who outstay their welcome? Is it you that normally gets stuck with the party bore? Been overlooked for promotion? If you're nodding at this point, the chances are that you're too nice for your own good. Described as "the first antidote to the national plague of overniceness," this book sets out to show you how to stand up for yourself and put your own needs first. Although much of the content of the book is reminiscent of the sort of stuff covered on assertiveness or self-esteem workshops, the authors have in the concept of "niceness" an original and very accessible vehicle for putting over their brand of effective relationship management.

» **Cooper, R. & Sawaf, A. (1997)** *Executive EQ*, **Orion Business Books, London.**

Daniel Goleman's best-selling *Emotional Intelligence*, published in 1996, claims that our emotions play a much greater role in thought, decision making and individual success than is commonly acknowledged. *Executive EQ* (the initials stand for emotional quotient) argues that emotional intelligence will be a new driving force in business. Whether this will prove to be the case is open to question – most organizations are still not noted for their emotional maturity – but this is a self-help book with enough business examples to give the idea credibility. Readers have the opportunity to map their own emotional intelligence by completing a questionnaire at the back of the book.

» **de Geus, A. (1997)** *The Living Company*, **Nicholas Brealey, London.**

Drawing on unpublished research conducted by Shell in the early 1980s, Arie de Geus – the man widely credited for originating the concept of the "learning organization" – believes that most companies fail because they focus too narrowly on financial performance and pay insufficient attention to themselves as communities of human beings with the potential to learn, adapt, and grow. The living company, he says, emphasizes knowledge rather than capital, and adaptability rather than core competencies. De Geus won the Edwin G. Booz prize for Most Insightful Management Book back in 1997 and so it is a little disappointing that his ideas have not yet broken through into the mainstream. Nonetheless, anybody with an interest in organizational learning will find something of value here.

» **Dixon, N.M. (1999)** *Dialogue at Work*, **Lemos & Crane, London.**

In this book, Nancy Dixon explores the contribution that dialog can make to a change management process. Dialog is the capacity of members of a team to suspend assumptions and enter into a genuine "thinking together" which leads to shared meaning and allows the group to discover insights not attainable individually. This contrasts with discussion, the "normal" way that we have of talking *at* each other, which literally means heaving our separate ideas back and forth in a kind of winner-takes-all competition. The book is relatively short but covers a lot of ground, always a good sign that an author not only knows her subject back-to-front, but also can express core ideas clearly and concisely. There is a good mix of theory, practical skills, and contemporary ideas on how to develop your organization's ability to dialogue, hence moving beyond individual learning to a more powerful form of group learning.

» **Donnellon, A. (1996) *Team Talk*, Harvard Business School Press, Boston, MA.**

Subtitled *The Power of Language in Team Dynamics,* this book uses anthropological and linguistic research techniques to focus on talk as the "medium through which team work is done and through which organizational and individual forces can be observed and analyzed." Given that language exchange is the primary way in which people swap information, make decisions, and formulate plans, Donnellon's book represents the long overdue entry of sociolinguistics into the field of management studies.

» **Fineman, S. (ed.) (1993) *Emotion in Organizations*, Sage, London.**

This ground-breaking book brings together a number of contributions from leading academics about how people can behave in companies and why this should be so. Not the easiest of reads, but it does make the point powerfully that a person's behavior always appears logical to that individual, no matter how irrational it might appear to others.

» **Gardner, H. (1996) *Leading Minds – An Anatomy of Leadership*, HarperCollins, New York.**

Gardner takes a variety of well-known leaders – as diverse as Margaret Thatcher and Gandhi – and tries to tease out what it is that made them so successful. He tops and tails his book with chapters on his theoretical framework and sandwiches the biographies in the middle. Gardner demonstrates brilliantly the qualities and experience needed by "leading minds," although less helpfully offers no practical guidance as to how readers might develop their own leadership skills.

» Handy, C. (2001) *The Elephant and the Flea*, Hutchinson, London.

In his latest book (and his best for some time), self-styled social philosopher Handy explores the business world of the twenty-first century, which he claims "will be a world of fleas and elephants, of large conglomerates and small individual entities, of large political and economic blocs and small countries." The smart thing, it seems, is to be the flea on the back of the elephant because a flea can be global as easily as one of the elephants but can more easily be swept away. Elephants are a guarantee of continuity but fleas provide the innovation. A fascinating premise, outlined lucidly by Handy in one of the first "must-reads" of this century.

» **Hochschild, A.R. (1998)** *The Time Bind: When Work becomes Home & Home becomes Work*, **Metropolitan Books, New York.**

Hochschild, a sociology professor at the University of California, Berkeley, spent three years interviewing hundreds of employees of a Fortune 500 company renowned for its family-friendly policies, to see how they reconciled their work and their home life. Using a series of vivid portraits, the author demonstrates the relentless and increasing pressure that is being placed on many of us, from the boardroom to the shop floor, to improve performance at work, show commitment to our organizations and perform our duties as parents. Hochschild's ground-breaking research exposes our crunch-time world and reveals how, after the first shift at work and the second at home, comes the third, and hardest, shift of repairing the damage created by the first two.

» **Jaques, E. (1996)** *Requisite Organization*, **2nd edn, Cason Hall, Gloucester, MA.**

Based on Jaques' latest research, this is a thorough revision of the original book published in 1989. *Requisite Organization* challenges many current assumptions about effective organizations, particularly in the field of hierarchy – of which Jaques is a fan. Some may find his theories indigestible, but for those who persist there is a wealth of challenging material that undermines much conventional organizational wisdom.

» **Kanigel, R. (1997)** *The One Best Way*, **Little Brown, New York.**

The One Best Way is an illuminating biography of Frederick W. Taylor, the efficiency expert and "the father of scientific management." Although he lived through little of it – he died in 1915, aged 59 – Taylor's influence on the twentieth century is unquestionable. Peter Drucker, for example, rates him alongside Freud and Darwin as a maker of the modern world. And despite its critics, Taylorism lives on, whether in the form of re-engineering (a direct descendant of scientific management), the continuing debate about the de-skilling of jobs, or the global standardization of companies like McDonald's. At 570 pages, the book is definitely top-heavy with detail. However, as an introduction to arguably the world's first management consultant, it makes fascinating reading.

» **Katzenbach, J. & Smith, D. (1993)** *The Wisdom of Teams*, **Harvard Business School Press, Boston, MA.**

According to Katzenbach and Smith – two senior McKinsey consultants – teams are "the primary building blocks of company performance." For this book, the authors talked with hundreds of people in more than 50 teams from 30 companies in a bid to discover what differentiates various levels of team performance, where and how teams work best, and how generally to enhance team effectiveness. Some of their findings are common sense – e.g. teams with a genuine commitment to performance goals and to a common purpose outperform those who place a greater emphasis on team-building. Others are, at face value, surprising (formal hierarchy, they say, is actually good for teams). In a chapter towards the end of the book they describe how top management can usefully support the development of a team-based culture.

» **Lipnack, J. & Stamps, J. (1997)** *Virtual teams*, **John Wiley & Sons, New York.**

According to Lipnack and Stamps, advances in communication technologies are having a dramatic impact on the nature of teamwork. Traditional, collocated teams are giving way to distributed, cross-boundary, virtual groups linked by technology and reaching across space, time, and organizational boundaries. Drawing on the experience of organizations like Hewlett-Packard and Motorola, they set out the factors that underpin successful virtual team performance, while at the same time warning that misunderstandings are more likely with virtual teams compared to their face-to-face counterparts and that more things are likely to go wrong.

» **Maslow, A. (1998)** *Maslow on Management*, **John Wiley & Sons, New York.**

Abraham Maslow remains one of the most widely known experts on human behavior and motivation. His psychological perspectives on management, such as the hierarchy of needs, are still studied today in business schools all over the world. Now, 37 years after its original publication, Maslow's most influential business book, *Eupsychian Management*, has been updated to include commentaries by some of today's management thinkers, who discuss the continuing relevance of his ideas. *Maslow on Management* is a stimulating but not always easy read that demonstrates clearly why Maslow was an unparalleled thinker and innovator in applying human behavior to the workplace.

» **Moore, J.F. (1996) *The Death of Competition*, HarperCollins, New York.**

Business as ecosystem – Moore explores the biological metaphor in great detail and with considerable insight. One of the first and arguably the best exploration of leadership and strategy in a future that Moore envisions will be characterized by organized chaos.

» **Peters, T. & Waterman, R. (1982) *In Search of Excellence*, Warner Books, New York.**

With the publication of *In Search of Excellence* some two decades ago, Tom Peters and co-author Bob Waterman changed the way organizations thought about themselves. Notions of embracing a paradoxical world of constant change, of providing exemplary customer service, and of the need for high-speed response are now mainstream corporate thinking, but during the mid-1980s, when at the peak of their fame, the challenge laid down by Peters and Waterman was enormous.

» **Pink, D. (2001) *Free Agent Nation: How America's New Independent Workers Are Transforming The Way We Live*, Warner Books, New York.**

Daniel Pink looks at the seismic changes occurring in the American workforce. He highlights the shift from "organization man" to "free agent worker." Pink defines free agents as "free from the bonds of a large institution, and agents of their own futures ... the new archetypes of work in America." A classic in the making.

» **Pitcher P. (1997) *The Drama of Leadership*, John Wiley & Sons, New York.**

Exploding a number of popular myths about leaders on the way, *The Drama of Leadership* is an insightful and passionate appeal to rethink the type of people that organizations will need at the helm in the twenty-first century. Relatively light on practical guidance though.

» **Ridderstråle, J. & Nordström, K. (2000)** *Funky Business: Talent Makes Capital Dance*, **Financial Times/Prentice Hall, London.**

On the face of it, a business book by two Swedish professors about how successful companies differ from their competitors doesn't sound like the most riveting of reads. But *Funky Business* is no dry theoretical tome; and authors Ridderstråle and Nordström are not your standard issue academics. Unless, that is, it's normal for Swedish business professors to shave their heads, wear leather trousers, describe themselves as funksters, and call their public appearances gigs rather than seminars. Funky management, for Nordström and Ridderstråle, means innovation, constant change and, especially, reliance on people as the main source of "sustainable uniqueness." This book draws extensively from rigorously researched data but presents its findings with wit and intelligence, reinforced with excellent examples.

» **Robbins, H. & Finley, M. (1997)** *Why Change Doesn't Work*, **Orion Books, London.**

According to Robbins and Finley, the most neglected aspect of the whole change process is the human factor. This is clear from their "seven unchangeable rules of change." Five of the seven rules feature people as the first word with the remaining two highlighting vision and imagination.

» People do what they perceive is in their best interest, thinking as rationally as circumstances allow them to think.

» People are not inherently anti-change. Most will, in fact, embrace initiatives provided the change has positive meaning for them.

» People thrive under creative challenge, but wilt under negative stress.

» People are different. No single "elegant solution" will address the entire breadth of these differences.

» People believe what they see. Actions do speak louder than words, and a history of previous deception octuples present suspicion.

» The way to make effective long-term change is to first visualize what you want to accomplish, and then inhabit this vision until it comes true.

» Change is an act of the imagination. Until the imagination is engaged, no important change can occur.

The optimal approach to managing change, they believe, is one which initially gains people's attention and starts them thinking, and which subsequently leverages people's knowledge and creativity to achieve successful and sustainable change. This is an exceptionally stimulating book, one that fizzes with ideas and insights, and one that should be read by anybody who would like their thinking about organizational change reinvigorated.

» **Schein, E.H. (1987)** *Process Consultation – Volume 2*, **Addison-Wesley, New York.**

One of the persistent dilemmas that faces any manager is when to help others figure out a solution by using facilitation skills and when to explicitly give advice or tell others what to do. This book, intended for relatively experienced consultants and managers, outlines the benefits of process consultation – Schein's facilitation model – as a viable means of getting things done. It clarifies the concept of process consultation as defined in the previous, more theoretical volume, *Process Consultation: Its Role in Organization Development* (1969), and introduces modifications and new ideas that elaborate on and have evolved beyond the material in the first volume. Included are such topics as initiating and managing change; intervention strategy; tactics and style; and emerging issues in process consultation. Volume 2 is a valuable and reasonably practical resource for anyone involved in the management of people.

» **Schwartz, P. & Gibb, B. (1999)** *When Good Companies Do Bad Things*, **John Wiley & Sons, Chichester, UK.**

In *When Good Companies Do Bad Things*, the authors discuss business ethics at companies such as Nestle, Texaco, Union Carbide, Nike, and Royal Dutch/Shell. They examine incidents involving each of these companies, and suggest alternative approaches to the actual damage control methods adopted by the organizations in question when they were faced with (often highly public) challenges to their reputations.

» **Senge, P. (1990)** *The Fifth Discipline*, **Business Books, New York.**

Senge's book was one of the first to popularize the concept of the learning organization. His five core disciplines that underpin the building of a learning community are personal mastery; mental models (the filters through which we view the world); shared vision; team learning; and systems thinking. The last of these, which Senge terms the "cornerstone discipline," is covered in 70 pages in a section that represents an excellent generalist introduction to the main concepts of systems thinking, a core skill in a globalized, networked economy.

» **Simmons, A. (1998) *Territorial Games*, Amacom, New York.**

This is a fascinating exploration of organizational turf wars – why they occur and what we can do about them. Simmons identifies and describes ten different territorial games that are enacted within organizations (see Chapter 6). She then goes on to examine what can be done to end turf wars at work, and to suggest a set of strategies by which the impact of territorial games can be defused.

» **Stewart, T.A. (1997) *Intellectual Capital: The New Wealth of Organizations*, Bantam Books, New York.**

This book has proved itself in the market place as the definitive guide to understanding and managing intangible assets. The author provides a framework, practical guide, and theory of the significance of intellectual capital (defined by Stewart as "packaged useful knowledge") which is a delight to read. In an age of lightweight books on the new information age, this book is a heavyweight which explains why intellectual capital will be the foundation of corporate success in the new century.

» **Weaver, R. & Farrell, J. (1997) *Managers as Facilitators*, Berrett Koehler, New York.**

According to Weaver and Farrell, successful managers must use facilitation skills to help people exercise the freedom to make decisions, respond quickly to customers, work together more effectively, and produce the results needed by their organizations. They say that to become a successful facilitator, one must recognize and use the four key elements of the facilitation model: task, self, group, and process. They explore each element in detail, and offer step-by-step guidance to applying the model to real work situations.

Managers as Facilitators is an excellent source of ideas to use as a team develops and changes. The chapter on change will give many readers insightful "a-has" of recognition as they reflect on organizational changes they have experienced. Real-world examples make the book accessible as well as practical, and a Quick Fix section offers excellent clues to solving everyday management problems.

ARTICLES

These are listed in date order, most recent first.

» Anon (2001) "Good to great," *Fast Company*, October.

Start with 1435 good companies. Examine their performance over 40 years. Find the 11 companies that became great. Now, here's how you can do it too.

» Brown, J.S. & Duguid, P. (2001) "Creativity vs structure: A useful tension," *Sloan Management Review*, Summer.

Great new ideas help only those organizations with the discipline and infrastructure needed to implement them.

» Pink, D.H. (2001) "Land of the free," *Fast Company*, May.

» Bonabeau, E. & Meyer, C. (2001) "Swarm intelligence: A whole new way to think about business," *Harvard Business Review*, May.

» Webber, A.M. (2001) "How business is a lot like life," *Fast Company*, April.

If you want your company to stay alive, then try running it like a living organism. The first rule of life is also the first rule of business: Adapt or die.

» Hansen, M.T. & von Oetinger, B. (2001) "Introducing T-shaped managers: Knowledge management's next generation," *Harvard Business Review*, March.

Most companies do a poor job of capitalizing on the wealth of expertise scattered across their organizations. The authors put forward something they call T-shaped management, which requires executives to share knowledge freely across their organization (the horizontal part of the "T"), while remaining committed to their individual business unit's performance (the vertical part).

» Fulmer, R.M., Gibbs, P.A. & Goldsmith, M. (2000) "Developing leaders: How winning companies keep on winning," *Sloan Management Review*, Fall.

» Mintzberg, H. & van der Heyden, L. (1999) "Organigraphs: Drawing how companies really work," *Harvard Business Review*, September-October.
» Nicholson, N. (1998) "How hardwired is human behavior," *Harvard Business Review*, July-August.

Evolutionary psychology asserts that human beings today retain the mentality of our Stone Age ancestors. We are, in other words, "hardwired" for certain attitudes and behaviors. If that is so, what are the implications for managers?

» Anon (1997) "Of soloists and session men," *Economist*, 22 February.

An exploration of the balance between individuality and fraternity among jazz musicians.

» Heifetz, R.A. & Laurie, D.L. (1997) "The work of leadership," *Harvard Business Review*, January-February.

For Heifetz and Laurie, leadership occurs only when those in responsible roles make happen what wouldn't have happened anyway. The authors call this adaptive work, in contrast to technical work, in which executives draw upon a repertoire of pre-existing solutions to address the problems at hand. They also divorce leadership from personality traits.

» Collins, J.C. & Porras, J.I. (1996) "Building your company's vision," *Harvard Business Review*, September-October.
» Kotter, J.P. (1995) "Leading change: Why transformation efforts fail," *Harvard Business Review*, March-April.
» Anon (1997) "The vision thing," *Economist*, 25 September.
» Stayer, R. (1990) "How I learned to let my workers lead," *Harvard Business Review*, November-December.

JOURNALS, MAGAZINES, AND WEBSITES

For readers wanting to keep up to date with developments in the strategy field, the following list of publications and Websites are worth dipping into on a regular basis:

Center for Business Innovation

A site managed by consultants Ernst and Young - the quality of the content varies but occasionally provokes thought.

www.businessinnovation.ey.com

The *Economist*

The best single source of information about what is happening in the world. A mainstream publication but one that will take on some big topics from time to time, and one whose take on the new economy is variably insightful and clear-eyed.

www.economist.com

Fast Company

The magazine is monthly and has been an essential read since it started up in 1996. Of late though, the content – whilst still excellent – has been swamped by increasing volumes of advertising. The companion Website is just about the best free site around on the future world of work (it also carries material not found in the magazine).

www.fastcompany.com/home.html

Financial Times

Of all the dailies, the *Financial Times* provides the best in-depth coverage of organization-related issues

www.ft.com

Harvard Business Review

The most authoritative business monthly on the block. Has tended in the past to be more mainstream than truly groundbreaking in its coverage of business issues. That said, *HBR* has responded well to the challenge to traditional business thinking posed by the new economy, and recent issues have generally contained two or three relevant articles. Also, if you are interested in getting the lowdown on forthcoming books from Harvard's publishing wing several months before publication, the magazine consistently trails major books with articles from the authors. The Website provides overview of contents of the magazine – no free articles but the executive summaries are there and they are often all you need.

www.hbsp.harvard.edu/home.html

The *Leadership and Organization Development Journal*

The *Leadership & Organization Development Journal* aims to provide penetrating insights into the expected qualities of leaders in the current climate. It presents research and views on making and developing dynamic leaders, how organizations can and will change, and how leaders can effect this. Contains some excellent links to free articles and information.

www.emeraldinsight.com/lodj.htm

Management Link

A one-stop shop containing links to more than 100 key management Websites.

www.inst.mgt.org.uk/external/mgt-link

People Management

The online magazine of the Chartered Institute of Personnel and Development.

www.peoplemanagement.co.uk

Sloan Management Review

Since its founding in 1959, MIT's *Sloan Management Review* has covered all management disciplines, although its particular emphasis these days is on corporate strategy, leadership, and management of technology and innovation. Over the years it has featured articles by the likes of Peter Senge, Lester Thurow, James Brian Quinn, Gary Hamel, Thomas Davenport, Christopher Bartlett, Sumantra Ghoshal, John Quelch, Henry Mintzberg, Max Bazerman, and Ed Lawler.

mitsloan.mit.edu (note no www)

Edschein.com

This site is dedicated to the life and work of Edgar Schein, widely acclaimed as one of the founders of the field of organizational psychology.

www.edschein.com

HR Network

This Website contains some excellent material about team development. It describes seven characteristics, depicted by the acronym PERFORM, that are necessary for a group to become a high performing team. The characteristics are Purpose and values; Empowerment;

Relationships and communication; Flexibility: Optimal productivity; Recognition and appreciation; and Morale.

   www.hrnetwork.co.uk

Imaginiz

This site is dedicated to the work and thinking of Gareth Morgan.

   www.imaginiz.com

Ten Steps to Making it Work

- » Leadership.
- » Decision-making.
- » The power of teams.
- » Managing conflict.
- » Innovation.
- » Emotional intelligence.
- » Managing external consultants.
- » Address the issues, not the culture.
- » Managing intellectual capital.
- » Change your organizational lenses.

"Optimism is a strategy for making a better future. Because unless you believe that the future can be better, it's unlikely you will step up and take responsibility for making it so. If you assume that there is no hope, you guarantee that there will be no hope. If you assume that there is an instinct for freedom, that there are opportunities to change things, there's a chance you may contribute to making a better world."[1]

Noam Chomsky

The following ten points don't attempt to represent absolutely the major priorities for your organization right now. Some of the points may be irrelevant to your organization and its marketplace; there may be other points not covered. So recognize the following as a set of generalized principles that will serve most organizations well most of the time.

These are the ten points:

1 Leadership
2 Decision making
3 The power of teams
4 Managing conflict
5 Innovation
6 Emotional intelligence
7 Managing external consultants
8 Address the issues, not the culture
9 Managing intellectual capital
10 Change your organizational lenses.

Let's take each in turn.

1. LEADERSHIP

Excellent leaders understand the Pygmalion Effect, namely that people behave the way they are treated: expect your team to fail and - sure enough - that's what will happen; treat them as competent, talented individuals and they'll live up to your expectations.

They also intuitively understand Buckminster Fuller's axiom that you never change things by fighting the existing reality, that what you have to do is build a new model that makes the existing model obsolete. In a world of work where the rules of the game are being re-shaped before our eyes, their ability to put their own stamp on things enables them to become masters of, and not victims of, circumstance.

Leadership lies at the heart of successful change. The leader carries the torch for the organization, ignites the passion for change within, and acts as a catalyst for that change. He or she is the ultimate custodian of the organizational vision. Leadership is sometimes referred to as the *temple of intentionality*, as it embodies the will to act within an organization. It is the element of leadership that is widely recognized when researchers ask groups to name great leaders. Groups often identify powerful political and military figures such as Churchill, Alexander the Great, Genghis Khan, Margaret Thatcher, Gandhi, Martin Luther King, Julius Caesar, Hitler (not all effective leaders are necessarily "good"), John F. Kennedy, and others who epitomize this will to act.

There is another equally important aspect of leadership; one which focuses on maintaining relationships among group members. This is often not recognized at first, although groups sometimes identify spiritual figures such as Jesus, Mother Teresa, and The Buddha among their list of great leaders. Nevertheless this aspect is fundamental to effective leadership, allowing the leader to sustain the people involved in the process of creating a *shared* vision for the organization.

We do not fully understand leadership. Some writers argue that leaders truly create the future, others that they are far more attuned than others to the *zeitgeist*, the spirit of the times.

Howard Gardner, a leading authority on leadership, argues that leaders are all those who "by word and/or personal example, markedly influence the behaviors, thoughts, and/or feelings of a significant number of their fellow human beings."[2] Gardner emphasizes the ability of leaders to tell or embody stories that speak to other people and describes a continuum of leadership that starts with indirect leadership, exerted through written work or other symbolic communication, and progresses to direct leadership of the sort exercised by world leaders through speeches and other means.

There is a great more that could be said about leadership. For our purpose, however, we need only make one final observation. At the heart of leadership there lies a paradox, which was captured succinctly by Lao Tsu:

The wicked leader is he who people despise.
The good leader is he who people revere.
The great leader is he who the people say, "We did it ourselves."

For 20 years, consultant and writer Richard Pascale was on the faculty of the Stanford Business School. He is now an associate Fellow of Oxford University. The following key points are adapted from a letter by Pascale that appeared in the *Harvard Business Review*.[3] He wrote in response to an article by Ronald Heifetz and Donald Laurie on leadership that was published in the January–February 1997 issue.

» Leadership occurs only when those in responsible roles consciously endeavor to make happen what wouldn't happen anyway. Heifetz and Laurie call this adaptive work, and it always occurs outside one's comfort zone. Adaptive work is in contrast to technical work, in which executives draw upon a repertoire of pre-existing solutions to address the problems at hand. Technical work is nothing to be ashamed of but it does not require leadership.

» At face value, the distinction between technical work and adaptive work is not difficult to comprehend. The trouble is, with "leadership" being so fashionable these days, many executives don't like to think that they are merely making happen what was going to happen anyway. The idea that most people who occupy executive positions are merely stewards of the inevitable is provocative.

» The authors' second radical idea is to divorce leadership from personality traits. Charisma, boldness, even the capacity to generate organizational purpose are absent from their model. Instead, the central theme shining through their work is mindfulness. They highlight the capacity to discern when traditional solutions are not likely to produce the desired results. That discernment must be followed not by the exercise of personality traits or hard-to-acquire skills but by the discipline necessary to enroll the organization in seeking new solutions.

2. DECISION-MAKING

When making business decisions, 88% of management admit to using gut feel over and above hard facts up to 75% of the time. 91% admit that they do not get enough thinking time, and 62% say that they do not get the right amount of information to make a decision.

Decision Making Survey 1997, *published by Business Objects*

Decision-making has been defined as the ability to decide on a course of action after due reflection. Making good quality decisions enables us to show that we can make a positive difference, that we are not merely intent on maintaining the status quo.

An article in *Fast Company* magazine[4] suggests four steps to making smarter decisions:

1 *Wait until the last minute – but not a minute later*. If you're not going to do anything differently tomorrow by making a decision today, then don't make it today. Situations change; markets shift. That's not an excuse to procrastinate. But the best decisions are just-in-time decisions.

2 *Don't be afraid to argue*. Conflict is good for an organization – as long as it's resolved quickly. Real leaders deal with conflict head-on. One way to make progress on a tough decision is to agree on what the question is. Agree on the wording and write it down. Debate often stems from having different ideas about what's being decided.

3 *Make the right decision, not the best decision.* People can spend months debating the "best" decision without actually arriving at any decision. Every decision involves risk. And if there are ten ways to do something, eight of them will probably work. So pick one of the eight and get going.

4 *Disagree – and then commit.* Not everyone gets a chance to decide, but everyone should have a chance to be heard. Without a doubt, the most vigorous debates yield the best thinking. But once a decision is made, you should not be able to tell who was for it and who was against it.

A Harvard Business School article[5] maintains that bad decisions can often be traced back to the way the decisions were made. For example, perhaps the alternatives were not clearly defined, the right information was not collected, the costs and benefits were not accurately weighed. But sometimes the fault lies not in the decision-making process but rather in the mind of the decision-maker. Here are eight psychological traps that are particularly likely to affect the way people make business decisions.

» The anchoring trap: this leads us to give disproportionate weight to the first information we receive.

» The status-quo trap: this biases us toward maintaining the current situation – even when better alternatives exist.

» The sunk-cost trap: this inclines us to perpetuate the mistakes of the past.

» The confirming-evidence trap: this leads us to seek out information supporting an existing predilection and to discount opposing information.

» The framing trap: this occurs when we misstate a problem, undermining the entire decision-making process.

» The overconfidence trap: this makes us overestimate the accuracy of our forecasts.

» The prudence trap: this leads us to be overcautious when we make estimates about uncertain events.

» The recallability trap: this leads us to give undue weight to recent, dramatic events.

3. THE POWER OF TEAMS

Working collaboratively is far more likely to deliver good results than working competitively. Somebody once wrote that moving from dependence to independence is a sign of growing up, but that moving from independence to interdependence is a sign of maturity.

There was a story in the papers in the late 1990s concerning one of the main Whitehall departments that used to run a course called "Getting the most out of your junior staff." One of the juniors objected to the title and as a consequence the course was renamed "Succeeding with teams." The content, needless to say, was identical.

If nothing else, this anecdote serves to demonstrate how potent the concept of "team" has become in recent times. According to Jon Katzenbach and Douglas Smith – two senior McKinsey consultants – teams are "the primary building blocks of company performance." For a book they wrote,[6] the two of them talked with hundreds of people in more than 50 teams from 30 companies in a bid to discover what differentiates various levels of team performance, where and how teams work best, and how generally to enhance team effectiveness. Some of their findings are common sense – e.g. teams with a genuine commitment to performance goals and to a common purpose outperform those who place a greater emphasis on teambuilding. Others are at face value surprising (formal hierarchy, they say, is actually good for teams).

More recently, Katzenbach has moved his focus up the organizational ladder. He believes that the best corporate leaders are those who actively shift in and out of team mode behind closed doors. The widely held view that teamwork is a *sine qua non* of organizational success is, he believes, fundamentally mistaken and has generated five myths about teamwork at the top, namely that:

» teamwork at the top will lead to team performance;
» top teams need to spend more time together building consensus;
» CEOs must change their personal style to obtain team performance;
» the senior group should function as a team whenever it is together; and
» teams at the top need to "set the example."

He maintains that the challenge for executives is to see through these myths and recognize when a team effort is needed and when a working group under single leadership is the more effective route to follow.

4. MANAGING CONFLICT

According to a *Harvard Business Review* article,[7] constructive conflict can actually enhance team performance and in turn achieve better decision-making. The article suggests five ways to achieve this.

1 Assemble a team with diverse ages, backgrounds and industry experience.
2 Meet frequently to build familiarity and mutual confidence.
3 Encourage team members to assume roles outside of their obvious functional responsibilities, and so discourage "turf war" thinking.
4 Apply multiple perspectives – role playing, putting yourself in the competitor's shoes, etc. This can enable a fresh view of the problem.
5 Actively and overtly manage conflict. Ensure that consensus is real and not just an indication of disengagement.

While at General Electric (GE), Jack Welch was known as an advocate of what he called "constructive contention." Elsewhere, writers like Richard Pascale have lent their support to the view that conflict can be the fuel of transformation.

5. INNOVATION

In a working world that grows ever more unpredictable, success will inevitably go to people who are naturally curious, willing to experiment, passionate about their work, and revolutionary in their thinking. Assuming that what works today will work tomorrow is a recipe for the scrapheap.

When it comes to assessing the contribution that his staff make to the business, Michael Eisner, head of the Disney Corporation, is unequivocal: "To me, the pursuit of ideas is the only thing that matters," he has said, "You can always find capable people to do almost anything else."

For a company, successful innovation requires a conscious and explicit commitment and inevitably involves risk. It is best achieved in a ''no blame'' culture which recognizes that mistakes and failures are the natural and inevitable bedfellows of successful ideas. An innovative organization is typically characterized by informality, the free flow of information, little hierarchy or bureaucracy, and creative interaction within small cross-functional teams and small business units.

Here are a few tips that will help to hone your capability in this area.

» Continually challenge conventional wisdom, and question all the time. Ask yourself, ''What does it mean?'' ''Why?'' ''What if?'' and ''How else could I do this?''
» Important questions are: ''Why does my organization exist?'' ''Why do we do things and have they any worthwhile purpose?'' ''What would we do differently if we started off again from scratch?'' ''Why don't we make the best use of our core competencies?'' ''Why don't we make it as easy as possible for our people to satisfy our customers?''

6. EMOTIONAL INTELLIGENCE

Emotional intelligence refers to the capacity for recognizing our own feelings and those of others, for motivating ourselves, and for managing emotions in ourselves and in our relationships. It describes abilities distinct from, but complementary to, academic intelligence. The emotionally intelligent manager finds it easier to network than their emotionally unintelligent peers, easier to build effective team relationships, and easier to acknowledge and deal with constructive criticism of their performance.

According to Daniel Goleman, the main popularizer of the concept, emotional intelligence embraces five emotional and social competencies.

» *Self-awareness*: knowing what we are feeling in the moment and using those preferences to guide our decision-making.
» *Self-regulation*: handling our emotions so that they facilitate rather than interfere with the task in hand.
» *Motivation*: using our deepest preferences to move and guide us toward our goals.
» *Empathy*: sensing what others are feeling, being able to take their perspective, and cultivating rapport with a broad range of people.

» *Social Skills*: handling emotions in relationships well and accurately reading social situations and networks; interacting smoothly; using these skills to persuade, lead, negotiate and settle disputes, etc.

In many organizations, emotional intelligence is most noticeable by its absence. Where people are not being emotionally intelligent, what you can see most commonly are individuals obsessively pursuing their own agendas. Self-interest rules.

7. MANAGING EXTERNAL CONSULTANTS

These days, organizations are bringing in external consultants in ever increasing numbers, particularly against a background of more and more activities being outsourced. This being so, the ability to make best and most cost-effective use of consultants becomes crucial. Here are some guidelines on how best to manage consultants, derived from *Dangerous Company* by James O'Shea and Charles Madigan.[8]

» Why are you doing this? Before you sit down to talk to a consulting firm, it would help to have some idea of what it is you want to achieve. The more clearly the goal is defined, the greater the chance of reaching it. If you don't know what you want to do, don't make the call.
» Having determined the goal, ask yourself whether you really need outsiders to help you reach it. Don't forget to assess the brilliance within your own company before you go trying to buy some from outside. Maybe you don't need an army of consultants.
» If you hire a consulting company, who will they send? Be ruthless in this part of the process. If you know the reputations of the partners, or if they display a special, tested expertise, demand that they personally pay good and frequent attention to your needs. Make it a part of the contract. If they are promising the best, make certain that is what shows up, and not an army of their latest graduate intake.
» What will it cost? (And how long will it take?) Avoid open-ended arrangements and vague promises. Go instead for specificity in contracts, including the dark parts about what happens if the consulting engagement doesn't work. Be tight with your money. Base payments on performance and on your satisfaction.

» Never give up control. The best consulting engagements do not take over your operations, they complement them. Make certain your own people retain control over everything, share in decision-making, and understand that for the duration of the contract, they are responsible and in charge.

» Consultants can shower down all kinds of havoc on a company. If you sense something is going wrong, confront it immediately and demand repairs. Consultants don't answer to boards of directors, but you do.

» Beware of glib talkers with books. The fact that someone can stack up case after case in which a practice seemed to work is no guarantee it will work for you. Insist on tailor-made consulting engagements that recognize the unique nature of your business. Don't be afraid to trim elegant proposals right down to their essence.

» Value your employees. One of the most common complaints about consultants is that they talk down to the locals or ignore their ideas. Long after the consultants leave, your staff will be on board. How they feel about the outsiders has a lot to do with whether the engagement will work. The best consulting companies know this and will go to great lengths to avoid morale problems.

» Measure the process. Make certain you have your own internal measure of how a procedure is progressing. Consulting companies do, and they generally try to make this a part of the process.

» If it's not broke, don't try to fix it. This is a great cliché, but more than an afterthought. It is in the consulting company's interest to find trouble where you see calm waters.

8. ADDRESS THE ISSUES, NOT THE CULTURE

What then can a company do if current cultural assumptions appear to be dysfunctional or out of alignment with environmental realities? Edgar Schein, a professor at the MIT Sloan School of Management, and probably the world's foremost authority on organizational culture, proposes the following set of steps.[9]

1 Start with what the "business problem" is. The organization must understand its mission or its primary task. This issue is not about culture, it is about the organization's reason to be at all.

2 Figure out what needs to be done strategically and tactically to solve the business problem

3 When there is clear consensus on what needs to be done, examine the existing culture to find out how present tacit assumptions would aid or hinder what needs to be done.

4 Focus on those cultural elements that will help you get to where you need to go. It is far easier to build up the strengths of the culture than to change those elements that are dysfunctional or weak.

5 Identify the culture carriers who see the new direction and feel comfortable moving in that direction. Empower specific employees and managers whose assumptions are already in line with the new strategy.

6 Build change teams around the new culture carriers.

7 Adjust the reward, incentive, and control systems to be aligned with the new desired strategy.

8 Ultimately the structures and routine processes of the organization must also be brought into alignment with the desired new directions.

Schein warns that all of this takes a great deal of time and energy on the part of many layers of management, many task forces and change teams. But the prerequisite for success is seeing a clear solution to a clear business problem.

9. MANAGING INTELLECTUAL CAPITAL

Time was when capital could be viewed in purely financial or physical terms – it showed up in the buildings and equipment owned, it could be found in the corporate balance sheets. In recent years, though, the search has been on for an altogether more elusive, intangible form of asset: intellectual capital.

Intellectual capital (defined by Thomas Stewart in his book *Intellectual Capital*[10] as "packaged useful knowledge") can be broken down into three areas.

» ***Human capital***: the knowledge that resides within the heads of employees that is relevant to the purpose of the organization. Human capital is formed and deployed, writes Stewart, "when more of the time and talent of the people who work in a company is devoted to activities that result in innovation." Human capital can grow in two ways: "when the organization uses more of what people know, and when people know more stuff that is useful to the organization." Unleashing the human capital resident in the organization requires "minimizing mindless tasks, meaningless paperwork, unproductive infighting."

» ***Customer capital***: the value of a company's ongoing relationships with the people or organizations to which it sells. Indicators of customer capital include market share, customer retention and defection rates, and profit per customer. Stewart's belief is that "customer capital is probably – and startlingly when you think about it – the worst managed of all intangible assets. Many businesses don't even know who their customers are."

» ***Structural capital***: the knowledge retained within the organization that becomes company property. Stewart calls this "knowledge that doesn't go home at night." Structural capital "belongs to the organization as a whole. It can be reproduced and shared." Examples of structural capital include technologies, inventions, publications, and business processes.

Understanding what intellectual capital amounts to is only part of the story for organizations. The real value comes in being able to capture and deploy it. To this end, Stewart offers the following 10 principles for managing intellectual capital.

» Companies don't own human and customer capital. Only by recognizing the shared nature of these assets can a company manage and profit from these assets.
» To create human capital it can use, a company needs to foster teamwork, communities of practice, and other social forms of learning.
» Organizational wealth is created around skills and talents that are proprietary and scarce. To manage and develop human capital companies must recognize unsentimentally that people with these talents are assets to invest in. Others are costs to be minimized.
» Structural assets (those intangible assets the company owns) are the easiest to manage but those that customers care least about.

» Move from amassing knowledge just-in-case to having information that customers need ready-to-hand, and that which they *might* need within reasonable reach.

» Information and knowledge can and should substitute for expensive physical and financial assets.

» Knowledge work is custom work.

» Every company should re-analyze the value chain of the industry that it participates in to see what information is most crucial.

» Focus on the flow of information, not the flow of materials.

» Human, structural, and customer capital work together. It is not enough to invest in people, systems, and customers separately. They can support each other or detract from each other.

10. CHANGE YOUR ORGANIZATIONAL LENSES

The more choices you have about you look at your organization, the richer and deeper your understanding of how it works and what might be undermining its performance.

Gareth Morgan suggests in his book *Images of Organization*,[11] that the use of metaphor is a form of organization analysis that can enrich appreciation. He talks, for example, about viewing the organization as a machine, as an organism, as a brain, or as a political system. Each of these metaphors provides a distinctive filter through which certain facets of the organization become more apparent.

The use of metaphors enables a way of thinking about organizations that can be quite releasing for mangers used to viewing the organization in a certain way. However, Morgan also takes pains to remind us that metaphors are not the experiences themselves, and so their value is bound to be limited.

NOTES

1 Chomsky, N. in an interview for *Wired*, January 1998.

2 Gardner, H. (1996) *Leading Minds: An Anatomy of Leadership*, Harper Collins, New York.

3 Letter by Richard Pascale, *Harvard Business Review*, June–July 1997.

4 In *Fast Company*, October 1998.

5 Hammond, J.S., Keeney, R.L. & Raiffa, H. (1998) "The hidden traps in decision-making," *Harvard Business Review*, September–October.

6 Katzenbach, J. & Smith, D. (1993) *The Wisdom of Teams*, Harvard Business School Press, Boston, MA.

7 Eisenhardt, K., Kahwajy, J. & Bourgeois, L.J. III (1997) 'How management teams can have a good fight,' *Harvard Business Review*, July–August.

8 O'Shea, J. & Madigan, C. (1999) *Dangerous Company*, Nicholas Brealey, London.

9 Schein, E. (1996) "Culture matters," *Demos Quarterly* **8**.

10 Stewart, T. (1997) *Intellectual Capital*, Doubleday, New York.

11 Morgan, G. (1986) *Image of Organization*, Sage, London.

Frequently Asked Questions (FAQs)

Q1: What is an organization?

A: There are numerous definitions. Some stress co-ordination of resources, some emphasize efficiency, while others focus on concepts like community and beliefs. Perhaps the most complete definition is that an organization is a social arrangement for achieving controlled performance in the pursuit of collective goals. See Chapter 2.

Q2: What is organizational behavior?

A: Many people – both theorists and practitioners – have offered their definitions of the term. A succinct definition of OB is that it is concerned with "the study of the structure, functioning, and performance of organizations, and the behavior of groups and individuals within them." A broader definition is offered by John Ivancevich and Michael Matteson, in their book *Organizational Behavior and Management*. They say that OB is about "the study of human behavior, attitudes, and performance within an organizational setting; drawing on theory, methods, and principles from such disciplines as psychology, sociology, and cultural anthropology to learn about *individual* perception, values, learning capabilities, and actions while working with *groups* and within the total *organization;* analyzing the external environment's effect on the organization and its human resources, missions, objectives and strategies.'' See Chapter 2.

Q3: What are the origins of organizational behavior?

A: Although the range of issues embraced by organizational behavior has been around as long as organizations themselves have existed, OB itself is a relatively young discipline. It is generally thought that the term was first coined by Fritz Roethlisberger in the late 1950s. In 1962, OB became a recognized subject area taught at Harvard Business School, and in 1970 the first academic Chairs in Organizational Behavior were appointed. See Chapter 3.

Q4: Who are the key figures in organizational behavior?

A: They are literally too numerous to mention. Four who have been particularly influential over the past 20 years have been Peter Senge (the learning organization and systems thinking), Jon Katzenbach (teams), Gareth Morgan (metaphors), and Geert Hofstede (culture). More recently, people like Ricardo Semler of Semco and Andy Law, Chairman at St Luke's advertising agency, have offered some interesting observations from a practitioner's perspective. See Chapters 2, 6 and 8.

Q5: Is there such a thing as an ideal set of organizational behaviors?

A: Absolutely not. There is no right or wrong set of behaviors, except in relation to what the organization is trying to achieve. It is totally appropriate that different organizations will have different values, operating patterns, decision-making processes, and so on. Organizations large or small, old or new, can be highly successful as long as they are tuned into the best practices that apply in their arena of activity. Often success is more about clarity of thinking and commitment than anything else. For some examples of successful organizations, see Chapter 7.

Q6: How does globalization impact on organizational behavior?

A: There are several implications for an organization, no matter what its size, location or industry sector. Most notably, globalization is intensifying levels of competition in many fields. See Chapter 5.

Q7: And what about the impact of new technology?

A: New technology has transformed the working practices of many organizations and has enabled a whole new body of organizational practices to come into being. See Chapter 4.

Q8: So where are organizations heading in the future?

A: Progressive, future-oriented organizations are always on the lookout for appropriate tools and lenses for improving future competitiveness. Charles Handy has plausibly described a future of "elephants" and "fleas" – very large corporations on the one hand, supported and serviced by external "fleas," small companies, perhaps comprising only one person, who will offer their expertise on a flexible basis. There will also be significant opportunities for companies of any size that can harness the potential of new and developing technology. See Chapter 6.

Q9: How valuable are case studies on organizations that have successfully changed the way they operate?

A: Case studies very rarely produce solutions that can be transplanted wholesale into a different company. Nonetheless, they will always throw up questions and may often suggest a way forward. See Chapter 3.

Q10: How can I find out more?

A: The problem is not accessing information about organizational behavior – there are literally thousands of books and articles around. The trick is to distinguish the useful from the irrelevant or derivative. For some recommendations, see Chapter 9.

Index

Printed and bound by CPI Group (UK) Ltd, Croydon, CR0 4YY

13/04/2025

14656462-0001